THE
LEPER SPY

The Story of an
Unlikely Hero of World War II

BEN MONTGOMERY

CHICAGO
REVIEW
PRESS

Published by Chicago Review Press Incorporated
814 North Franklin Street
Chicago, Illinois 60610
ISBN 978-1-61373-430-8

Library of Congress Cataloging-in-Publication Data
Names: Montgomery, Ben, author.
Title: The leper spy : the story of an unlikely hero of World War II / Ben
    Montgomery.
Description: Chicago : CRP, [2016] | Includes index.
Identifiers: LCCN 2016002542| ISBN 9781613734308 (cloth : alk. paper) | ISBN
    9781613734339 (epub) | ISBN 9781613734322 (kindle)
Subjects: LCSH: Philippines—History—Japanese occupation,
    1942–1945—Biography. | World War, 1939-1945—Underground
    movements—Philippines. | Guerrero, Josefina.
Classification: LCC D802.P5 M66 2016 | DDC 940.54/8673092—dc23 LC
record available at http://lccn.loc.gov/2016002542

Interior design: Jonathan Hahn
Map design: Chris Erichsen

Printed in the United States of America
5 4 3 2 1

For my mother, Donna

One life is all we have, and we live it as we believe in living it, and then it's gone. But to surrender what you are, and live without belief—that's more terrible than dying—more terrible than dying young.

—Joan of Arc, in *Joan of Lorraine* by Maxwell Anderson

Lord, if thou wilt, thou canst make me clean.

—Gospel of Matthew

CONTENTS

INTRODUCTION

The End

Washington, DC

In the last years, when she was living quiet and alone in the bustling capital of a country that had forgotten who she was and what she had done, she never spoke of the war. She kept the stories inside her head. No more bullets bit the dirt at her feet, and the flashbulbs had long since faded. Her few friends around town had no idea that she had once walked unflinching through cross fire half a world away, helping the fallen to their feet and closing the eyelids of the dead. They never knew the diminutive woman did something so daring that a US Army major general pinned a medal to her breast and said she had "more courage than that of a soldier on the field of battle" and that a Jesuit priest called her "one of the greatest heroes of the war." They would ask where she was from, and she'd tell them she was born inside an airplane high over the Pacific, or in San Francisco. Nothing more. No one even knew her real name.

Her posture was perfect, but she was tiny and easy to miss on the broad boulevards of Washington, DC, the lines of taillights stretching forever past her, the sidewalks a two-way stream of people trying to get somewhere else. She'd dress in a black skirt and plain white blouse and pull on a long coat and slip out of her apartment on New Hampshire Avenue and walk a few blocks in the fading sun to the grand John F. Kennedy Center for the Performing Arts, on the east bank of the Potomac, where she was Joey Leaumax, usher, volunteer. She'd show patrons to their seats with an anonymous smile, then disappear into the shadows to let the music wash over her.

That's why she was here, the music. She was a plain person, but she liked to say that the plain is always attracted to the beautiful. She never played an instrument, but she was raised on classical, heard it in her sleep, and it conjured images of her childhood, happy and peaceful, before the war, before her affliction, before she had to disappear in order to live. Her secret ambition had always been to visit all the places where she could embrace music: Carnegie Hall, the Metropolitan Opera House, the Hollywood Bowl. She fed her soul on concertos for piano and violin. She loved Chopin, Beethoven, Debussy, Saint-Saëns, Tchaikovsky. Humperdinck's *Hänsel and Gretel*. Mendelssohn's *A Midsummer Night's Dream*. Ravel's *Daphnis et Chloé*. Her favorite was Brahms—so soothing, like a journey into a land of magic dreams. She was especially fond of his Symphony no. 1 in C Minor. Of the four movements, she liked the second best of all. She felt like it was pregnant with unspoken yearnings, secret desires, until finally it broke into the third, the allegretto, so alive and intense until it reached the finale and the air exploded with music and excitement, like the sudden appearance of a white-hot sun after a rainstorm.

To find the music, she had to travel halfway around the world, then battle the great bureaucracy of the US government, then ultimately disappear into the roving citizenry. But finally. She would close her eyes and lose herself in the sound and at once see her mother and her daughter, whom she had left behind. Her brown-eyed little girl, a stranger now.

Those times were past and sealed in a box in her mind, and she would let them out to run and play up the crescendo.

She was Joey now. She had a simple apartment overflowing with books and a compact disc player and recent memories of a job as a clerk at the Gold and Silver Institutes, where she typed letters, her eyes straining behind thick glasses. She was always giving her things away, foisting books upon her visitors, who always felt bad because she had so little to give. She walked to Mass every day at St. Stephen Martyr and took the body and blood of Christ into her mouth, a sacred and consistent act, then walked home to be alone.

When her heart finally gave out a little after five o'clock on the morning of June 18, 1996, there was no grieving or gnashing of teeth. She left behind modest home furnishings; some costume jewelry; 850 books; two bags of used foreign stamps; foreign banknotes and traveler's checks; some vinyl records; many autographed ballet, opera, and theater posters; photos and Playbills; and a simple handwritten will and testament, leaving the little money she had after her debts were settled—about $5,000—to a handful of friends. Those trying to settle her affairs also found a mystery.

They found address books that, quite curiously, contained only the names of friends she had made starting in the 1970s, none from before. In calling these friends to alert them of Joey's death, no one seemed to know anything about her parents or when or where she was born. Among her possessions, there were no photographs taken prior to the late 1960s and no personal documents with an earlier date. Her passport said her place of birth was Manila, in the Philippine Islands, but none of her friends had ever heard that. She listed her year of birth as 1917, 1927, and 1937 on various documents. Her studio apartment was packed with years of catalogs, newspaper clippings, and correspondence, but there was nothing among her possessions to suggest she had ever been married or had a family. The friends assumed she was born in 1927 and had never married. Her death certificate and obituary would reflect the errors.

At her funeral a man read "Desiderata," and they buried her ashes in a box in a marble wall inside a chapel at Mount Olivet Cemetery, on the east side of the city. The funeral was well attended, and her obituary ran in the *Washington Post* beneath one for a money manager and above one for a chef, on June 28, 1996:

JOEY GUERRERO LEAUMAX

KENNEDY CENTER USHER

Joey Guerrero Leaumax, 68, a retired secretary who had worked as an usher at the Kennedy Center for the last 17 years, died of cardiopulmonary arrest June 18 at George Washington University Medical Center.

Ms. Leaumax, who had lived in Washington since 1977, was a secretary in the publications department of the Gold and Silver Institutes in Washington from 1977 until her retirement in 1990.

She was born in Manila and graduated from San Francisco State University. She received a master's degree in Spanish literature from Middlebury College, then spent four years as a Peace Corps volunteer, teaching English, music, and drawing to children and adults in Niger, Colombia, and El Salvador.

She was a member of St. Stephen-Martyr Catholic Church in Washington.

She leaves no immediate survivors.

A week after the obituary ran, a man called Joey's friend who had made the funeral arrangements. The man said he had known Joey Leaumax by a different name fifty years ago, in southern Louisiana. He told an astonishing story of a previous chapter of her life, unknown to her friends for the past thirty years.

This, of course, is the end of the story, but it's the best place to begin.

1

EVERYTHING IS IN READINESS

If you looked down on the cluster of 7,107 Philippine Islands from a Mitsubishi G4M bomber in the 1940s, you might see the profile of a stoop-shouldered old woman with her arms bent and her hands drawn up in prayer. Her face, the largest island, would be Luzon, and at the back of her throat sat Manila, the Pearl of the Orient, a bustling Asian city with a unique and diverse cultural tapestry shaped by the indigenous Tagalog Filipino, more than three hundred years of Spanish rule and, more recently, forty years of American occupation. The capital city was headquarters for American interests in the Orient, and the four decades of occupation had transformed Manila from a sleepy Spanish city into a thriving metropolis. Add to the mix a bunch of Chinese and Japanese migrants and Scottish and German traders who made Manila their home, and the city's cultural web connected it to three different continents and an international heritage. The only facet of culture that wasn't diverse was religion. The Spanish Catholic missions and educational system had converted generations upon generations, leaving few who didn't long for the body and blood of Jesus Christ.

Between the deep blue of Manila Bay and the thick jungle there grew high-rise buildings, apartment complexes, shopping centers, and hotels and beyond those, fish farms and rice paddies and the brown thatched roofs of bamboo houses. The mist that settled low upon the mountains ringing the city gave it an exotic feel. To the southwest, in the mouth of the ship-spackled bay, rose the rock island of Corregidor and a bit to the north stood the knuckled knobs of the Bataan Peninsula, behind which the sun disappeared each day.

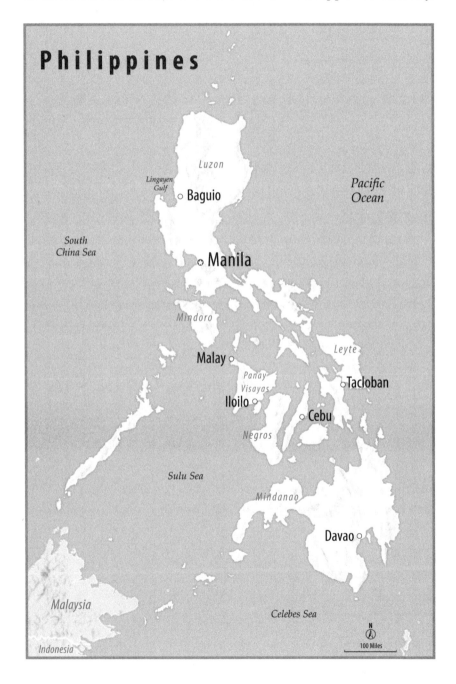

On hot nights the teenagers would drag their portable phonographs down to the seawall on the Vito Cruz corner, opposite the Casa Manana, and stomp to the music until sweat soaked their shirts. The street vendors sold sweet *halo-halo* from their carts, click-clacking down the paved roads, while river gypsies poled their *cascos* though the choking boat traffic on the Pasig. The bazaars were always packed with customers searching through straw hats and practical clay pottery, and the Escolta, the busiest boulevard, was a constant flurry of activity, the men darting through automobile and carriage traffic in white suits and the women sauntering in the heat. Inside the clubs, bodies pulsed every expression, displaying the blending of cultures: the tango, the flamenco, the waltz, the jive. It was a beautiful life, and though relatively short, the overlay of friendly American influence had left an impression. Most Filipinos felt, in some small way, like they were Americans.

The young commonwealth was on the cusp of independence after four hundred years of foreign rule, and the city was filled with a palpable anxiety. The United States was helping lift the Philippines to its feet, and at the head of that effort was a man who was pacing back and forth on the long sixth-floor balcony of the Manila Hotel, high above Dewey Boulevard.

Douglas MacArthur was born on a military base in Little Rock, Arkansas, the son of a Civil War hero. He learned how to ride and shoot before he learned how to read and write. He had been valedictorian at West Texas Military Academy, where he played quarterback and shortstop, and first in his class at West Point, and first captain, too. He had been the youngest major general in the US Army, the first American army officer ever to become a field marshal, and the first American to be a four-star general twice.

He smoked a corncob pipe, dressed loud, and wore swagger like cologne. His spine was straight as a flagpole. He had served as chief of staff in the War Department under Franklin Delano Roosevelt, but by 1934, near the sunset of his four-year term, developments in the Far East had grown interesting. The Japanese had conquered Manchuria, and Congress passed an act granting commonwealth status to the Philippines, now on its way to full independence, which would come in 1946. The exuberant leader of the Nacionalista Party, Manuel Quezon, was favored to be the new president of the independent Philippines, and he was working to establish a military to protect the islands. He leaned on MacArthur for help.

The general had served in the Philippines before, the first stint starting in 1903, the second in 1922, and the third later that decade. He knew the islands. He loved them. He also knew that politics in Washington were tumultuous. When FDR was adamant about cutting the War Department budget by 51 percent to pull the federal government out of the red, MacArthur stared down the president. "When we lose the next war, and an American boy with an enemy bayonet through his belly and an enemy foot on his dying throat spits out his last curse, I want the name not to be MacArthur, but Roosevelt," he said, voice trembling. He told the president he was resigning as chief of staff. As he turned to leave, FDR stopped him. "Don't be foolish, Douglas," the president said. "You and the budget must get together on this." Outside, MacArthur vomited on the steps of the White House.

Now he was in Manila. His family occupied the six-room penthouse atop the air-conditioned hotel, where he walked miles on the balcony overlooking the bay, Bataan, and Corregidor, wearing his West Point dressing gown and swinging a cane. He had been appointed field marshal in 1936, during a ceremony at Malacañang Palace, where the commonwealth's first lady, Aurora Quezon, presented him with a golden baton. He had become the highest-paid professional soldier in the world and often referred to himself in the third person. Nonetheless, he inspired awe on the streets of Manila. Filipinos loved MacArthur. He spoke to them with respect and came across as a sort of father figure, a protectorate. They saw him at the theaters, watching *The Great Ziegfeld* or *A Tale of Two Cities*, and at social affairs and cocktail parties. It also appealed to the heavily Catholic population that he seemed morally centered and rarely finished a gimlet.

MacArthur, meanwhile, was worried about defending the islands. The first measure Quezon put before his new legislature in 1935 had been a defense bill, but it took two years before the first twenty thousand draftees showed up at training camps, and then it was learned that they spoke eight languages in eighty-seven dialects. And a fifth of them were illiterate.

Nonetheless, MacArthur maintained that the strategically important islands—"the key that unlocks the door to the Pacific," as he called them—were defensible, even if they had more total coastline than the United States and were just one thousand miles from Nagasaki while they were seven thousand miles from San Francisco. He called for the formation of a Filipino navy that would man torpedo boats, for 250 aircraft, and for an army force of four hundred thousand Filipinos. "We're going to make it so very expensive for any nation to attack these islands that no nation will try it," he said. What's more, he regarded Japanese soldiers and pilots as inferior to red-blooded Americans. He knew the Japanese had been whipped by the Soviets during border clashes in 1938 and '39 and that they weren't able to defeat the peasant militias of China after three years of fighting.

But his war plan needed funding, and every indication was that Washington was iffy with support, at best. The War Department failed to allot money so MacArthur could pay his draftees a pittance. The Filipino trainees were issued pith helmets and shoes that fell apart during exercises, and they were armed with ancient Enfield rifles. As the war churned toward fury elsewhere, the War Department began reassessing plans in the Pacific. The Orange Plan, under which the US armed forces had been operating, suddenly felt outdated because it assumed a war between just two world powers. An updated plan drafted in June 1941 proposed abandoning the Philippines to Japan or defending it without additional military support, so the US effort could focus on defeating Italy and Germany.

July had brought a rapid turn of events. American scout planes were reporting large Japanese troop transports moving south. The

Japanese had seized nearly every port in China. They also were filling bases in French Indochina. Roosevelt watched Tokyo closely. He was well aware of the rising nationalism in Japan, laid bare in the Japanese army newspaper *Sin Shun Pao*, which demanded that the Japanese deliver the United States "a smashing blow." "We hate the United States, which forgets humane justice," the paper wrote. "The time will come when either we will swallow up the United States or the United States will swallow us."

"Awaken Asiatic people!" it continued. "We must speed up military and diplomatic measures by which we can crush Anglo-American efforts to obstruct the new order."

The new order the piece referred to was also known as the Greater East Asia Co-prosperity Sphere, which wasn't all that different from the concept of the Third Reich in Europe. It was a military exploitation of a nonmilitary idea. Original theorists coined the term to suggest Asia should be free from colonial powers through peaceful means. But nationalists had other ideas, as did the military, which hijacked the slogan and used its propaganda machine to bend the term to mean an Asia free from colonial powers, peace be damned. The push was on to fight and reclaim Anglo-occupied territories for Asian people.

On July 26, 1941, Roosevelt pushed back with an order that froze Japan's assets, clamping a sweeping control over all economic intercourse between the countries, including ships and silk and cash. He merged American and Filipino troops into one army, and MacArthur was the man who would lead them.

"By God, it was destiny that brought me here," the general said of his return to active duty.

In August, the United States stopped selling oil to Japan.

In September, after the American warship *Greer* was fired upon by a German submarine, FDR, his wife by his side on the first floor of the White House, gave the navy orders to shoot on sight any suspected Axis raiders in open water that America deemed vital to its defense. "We have sought no shooting war with Hitler, and don't seek it now," he told the American public. "But neither do we want peace so much that we are willing to pay for it by permitting him to attack our naval and merchant ships while they are on legitimate business." Some in Congress shot back, calling the order an unofficial declaration of war. An investigation into the USS *Greer* incident was launched by an isolationist US senator, but by then the footfalls toward a fight seemed imminent.

In October, as Russia pounded back against Germany in the west, surging and retreating, Japan began claiming that the US and British forces were trying to "encircle" the country, and the newspapers were filled with stories that war was likely at any time. American intelligence reports suggested the military group in Japan was on the ascendancy. Texas senator Tom Connally, chairman of the Senate Foreign Relations Committee, was worried that Japan was poised to strike the United States. He read the tea leaves. "It is within the bounds of possibility that we will have trouble with Japan," he told reporters. "In the present situation, anything could happen. If Japan decides that Germany is on top of Russia, she might try to interfere with our shipments of equipment to Russia. Her policy toward us certainly will be hooked up with the German military effort in Russia." Japan, he said, "would like to get something out of this war."

Just days later, the Nazis took Bryansk in their advance on Moscow, despite heavy losses in the snowy fields of Russia. The Reds advanced fresh troops constantly in order to stop the surge.

A week after the fall of Bryansk, on October 17, a strongly pro-Axis and heavily militarized faction took over in Japan, unseating moderate premier Prince Fumimaro Konoe, primarily because he hadn't reached an agreement during peace talks with the United States. The takeover came as such a shock that FDR canceled a cabinet meeting and called together his top military advisors: the secretary of state, the secretary of war, the secretary of the navy, the army chief of staff, and the chief of naval operations. Their meeting was so private that none of them spoke a word to reporters afterward.

Two days later, FDR announced he had adopted a wait-and-see policy to give the United States time to determine what the newly empowered Japanese military leaders were going to do. Meanwhile, Japanese leaders were making belligerent statements in the foreign press. The spokesman for the Japanese navy said they were "itching for action." George Norris, a Progressive Republican turned Independent from Nebraska, didn't like the way things were shaping up. "Like Hitler," he said, "the Japs believe that they are a superior race destined to rule the world. They have no friendship for the United States and will turn on us when they think it is to their interest."

In Manila, MacArthur was trying to make the best of what he had. He didn't expect an attack until April 1942, at the earliest, so he began ramping up defense installations. An $8 million airfield construction project gave the islands about forty finished airfields and an impressive concentration of warplanes. When a shipment of American B-17s flew over Manila on the way to Clark Field, the city cheered. The residents of working-class Tondo packed the streets to watch a parade of M3A1 tanks roll through, bound for Fort Stotsenburg.

By the end of October 1941, the rhetoric was fevered. The new Japanese premier, Gen. Hideki Tojo, said that Japan "must go on and develop in ever expanding progress—there is no retreat!"

"If Japan's hundred millions merge and go forward, nothing can stop us," he said. "Wars can be fought with ease."

On October 31, Halloween, a German U-boat torpedoed the USS *Reuben James*, which was on neutrality patrol near Iceland, the first sinking of an American destroyer by the Nazis. The ambush killed more than one hundred men. German chancellor Adolf Hitler's spin the following day, that the United States had attacked the submarine, was viewed as an attempt to pull Japan into the war. And it was followed by increasingly hostile rhetoric in the Japanese press.

On December 5, just as a group of educated Japanese civilians began an effort to convince the government to appoint a commission to try to solve the Pacific deadlock, President Roosevelt learned of the massing of Japanese troops in French Indochina. He called for an explanation. Two of Tokyo's envoys, Ambassadors Kichisaburo Nomura and Saburo Kurusu, showed up at the diplomatic entrance to the Department of State.

News cameras flashed as the two walked in, smiling blandly. They were ushered into the office of Cordell Hull, the Tennessean who had been secretary of state since 1933. The two met with Hull for twenty-five minutes. The United States was demanding that Japan sign a nonaggression pact and evacuate China and Indochina or its assets would remain frozen. Japan wanted America to halt its naval expansion in the western Pacific. Talks quickly broke down, and the envoys left Hull with a terse 150-word response from Tokyo, saying Japan was only reacting to aggressive Chinese troop movement: "As a natural sequence of this step, certain movements have been made among the troops stationed in the southern part of the said territory. It seems that an exaggerated report has been made of these movements. It should be added that no measure has been taken on the part of the Japanese government that may transgress the stipulations of the protocol of joint defense between Japan and France."

The War Department cabled MacArthur, saying, "Hostile action possible at any moment" and that "the United States desires that Japan commit the first overt act."

"Everything is in readiness," MacArthur replied.

It was not.

Lookouts sighted aircraft north of Manila, near Clark Field.

The next day, a Japanese reconnaissance plane was spotted in the sky.

The next day, at dawn, planes appeared once again, dark spots in the clouds above a peaceful island.

Later, MacArthur would write, "I prepared my meager forces, to counter as best I might, the attack that I knew would come from the north, swiftly, fiercely, and without warning."

On the night of December 7, all of Manila seemed to be partying. The Feast of the Immaculate Conception, the most important event on the calendar, the celebration of the Blessed Virgin Mary receiving the Messiah, was the next day. So the boys and girls danced the night away at the University of the Philippines. There were cocktail parties in Malate and jam sessions in Tondo. The twelve hundred men of the Twenty-Seventh Bombardment Group crammed into the Manila Hotel to celebrate their brigadier general's birthday. As they poured drinks and lit cigarettes, the Empire of the Sun was preparing for war.

2

FOOLS

The cadets stood in rigid formation on the reviewing grounds, their spines unbowed, rifles at their sides. Father John Fidelis Hurley was shown to his seat, a few feet from the podium erected for his friend the president. He recognized familiar faces in the crowd, practically all the ranking officials of the Commonwealth of the Philippines—Supreme Court justices, congressmen, senators, cabinet members. Beyond them sat thousands, here to watch the formal military review of the young men in the Reserve Officers' Training Corp (ROTC) at the University of the Philippines.

Hurley, the powerfully built superior of the Jesuit mission since 1936, was friendly with most of the politicians, even if he sparred with them occasionally. Some even attended Sunday Mass at the college he ran, the Ateneo de Manila. In a country where 90 percent of citizens were Catholic, the line between church and state, if such a line even existed, was blurry.

Hurley had come on the advice of a friend, a priest who organized the chaplain corps for the Philippine Army. He told Hurley the day would be unusual, that President Manuel Quezon seemed heavily burdened lately and had spent the week nervously preparing his address.

As the cadets finished their drills without incident, Hurley noticed the air was cool and the sky cloudy. It smelled like rain.

When Quezon approached the podium to give his speech, the sky opened, and a hard, drenching downpour fell. The cadets broke ranks without orders and sprinted for cover. Quezon was angry and bellowed at them, and the boys sheepishly returned.

The president clearly had a prepared speech, but he shoved the papers aside and leaned on the podium, his expression stern. "I am here to make a public confession of my first failure in public life," he said. A suppressed laugh rose from the crowd. Quezon was not joking. "If bombs start falling in Manila next week . . ."

Hurley couldn't hear what the president said next, because laughter thundered from the crowd. Hurley saw fury in Quezon's eyes. "You fools!" he shouted. The crowd fell silent. "If bombs start falling in Manila next week, then take the traitors and hang them to the nearest lamppost." Quezon continued, trying to warn them that war was coming at any moment and nobody was ready.

Hurley had never seen a man so sincerely honest, but the crowd reacted with incredulity. Even the cadets. They didn't know that Quezon had spent weeks complaining to US president Franklin Roosevelt about the weak defenses in the islands, or that Quezon had felt the need to tell his countrymen that war was coming when Roosevelt had begged him not to for fear it would upset the delicate international situation. He had defied Roosevelt out of a sense of duty to his people, and they had laughed.

3

FAMILY

Maybe war was coming, but there was always one last dance to be shared at the Silver Slipper, one last Hollywood film at the Ideal or the Lyric cinemas on Escolta, one last sweaty swing at the Santa Ana Cabaret, the largest in the Pacific. This was peacetime in the Philippine Islands for a generation that had never known war. And in the folds of that intoxicating happiness, a young man and a young woman found love.

The young woman was petite, with narrow shoulders and slender arms. She parted her curly black hair on the left, and the ringlets fell down past her dark eyes to her shoulders. Her pedigree did not match his. Born on August 5, 1917, Josefina Veluya grew up outside Manila, to the southeast, in the rural province of Lucban. Her name meant "God shall add." As a child, the girl they called Joey idolized Joan of Arc.

She'd read the story of the young warrior in a book, and it awoke in her a powerful defiance. She used to pretend to be the martyr saint, pretend she could hear the voice of God, comforting her and commanding her in battle. She got bored pretending and asked her brother if he could pretend to be the voices, which always made her laugh.

Earnestly, she prayed each day that God would let her be a nun and live a cloistered life in service and reflection. When her parents both died unexpectedly, the Good Shepherd Sisters convent seemed like a natural place for her, but her body was attacked by tuberculosis and the nuns did not have the capacity to give her care.

She was taken in by her grandparents, who owned a coconut plantation, and she soon regained her health. She was then sent to live with an uncle in Manila for schooling, and he enrolled her in studies at the nearby convent, where her new classmates were children from wealthy families. She was well read, spoke proper English, and adored all things beautiful—art, poetry, and especially music. When her inheritance ran low, she started working to pay her own tuition. At the convent, she was a member of every athletic team—swimming, baseball, basketball. She was elected president of the student council.

Renato Maria Guerrero was a rising medical student, a scion of one of the most distinguished families in the Philippines, with deep roots in intellectual society in the city. He came from painters, lawyers, poets, journalists, and doctors, many of them revolutionaries as well. His father, Manuel Severino Guerrero, was the most renowned doctor of his time. People said he had a clinical eye, because he could diagnose a man's illness simply by studying his outward appearance. He taught medicine at the University of Santo Tomas, wrote for *La Republica Filipina* and *La Opinion*, and published a short story collection on the side. His reputation connected him to Manila's elite, men and women whose names would live on the city's infrastructure, its signposts and buildings, long after they were gone.

The doctor gave his children all the comforts his wealth afforded. He bought them the latest gadgets from shops like La Puerta del Sol, white rolls of linen, silverware of all kinds, wine and chocolates and Piña hams. The family lived in a two-story house facing Plaza Ferguson and owned two cars and a horse. In the summers, the doctor rented a large nipa house in Antipolo, not far from the church. He bought his children one of the first gramophones in the islands, the kind you had to wind by hand after each record. The children went to sleep at night listening to Caruso, Chaliapin, Tetrazzini, Wagner, Beethoven. Young Renato, the eldest of the children, studied piano and practiced until he became a brilliant player. His favorites were the Debussy pieces.

The family was the wealthiest of all the Ermita Guerreros, so refined that the children were forbidden to eat with their hands, which was customary in the culture, or to converse in Tagalog, the native tongue.

They were pious, too, and each child was baptized almost immediately after birth. The elders used to ask the children, "Why were you born?" And the answer they expected was "To know, serve, obey, and love God on earth and be happy with Him in heaven." They learned the catechism, memorized Our Father, Hail Mary, and the Apostles' Creed, and took Communion daily, rain or shine.

Their father had a quirk, though, in that he was terrified of germs and communicable diseases. He rarely opened doors unless he had a handkerchief or napkin, and he was constantly washing his hands.

When he fell ill from stomach cancer in 1919, he sent Renato, twelve at the time, to fetch a priest, and his sick room was soon occupied by the upper crust of Manila. He received the sacred viaticum, the *extremaunción*, and the plenary indulgence for the time of death. When he had finished, his children approached him one at a time.

"You don't understand anything about death," he told Manuel II, who was holding a toy.

"This one is undefinable," he said about Wilfredo, who would become perhaps the greatest playwright in the Pacific. "God will take care of you, my son."

He called Renato closer.

"You, being the eldest, must be like the father of your younger brothers," he said.

He blessed them all, and the visitors in his room began to weep. He spoke softly of the Virgin Mary and then died. His wife was so sick with grief that she would wear black every day for the remaining thirty-nine years of her life.

Renato helped his mother and aunts raise his brothers. His father left the family a ten-thousand-peso insurance policy, two cars, the house, and all his possessions, but because the children were all minors, their mother could not spend any money without permission from the family's lawyer. She eventually sold both cars, moved her children into a rental flat, and rented their large home to Americans. She kept her sons fed off the monthly rental income.

The boys attended the Ateneo de Manila, inside the walls of the Spanish city of Intramuros, where they sang in the chorus in lieu of paying tuition. All but Renato, whose high school and college were paid for by Dr. Gregorio Singian, a famous surgeon. It was the Jesuit priests at the Ateneo who introduced him to Joey.

It wasn't long before she had shortened his name to Rene. They took long strolls together down the Escolta, in the thick and warm evenings. He fell hard for her. He liked what he called her snub nose, which turned up ever so slightly, and her high cheeks. She carried herself gracefully but could also be a clown.

They married on April 21, 1934. He was twenty-six and she was just sixteen and they moved into a lovely home on Florida Street in the Ermita district of Manila. His studies and hospital work kept him away from home, busy as he was on the ward at St. Paul's Hospital in the old walled city of Intramuros. But the job afforded them a long and sleek Buick, a driver, and two live-in maids.

Less than two years after their marriage, Joey learned she was pregnant. Rene was now a doctor, so Joey began to plan for a home birth. On November 6, 1936, she gave birth to a baby girl, and they named her Cynthia. She had big brown eyes and dark chestnut hair and beautiful white skin. Joey thought the child took after her own mother, who was Spanish. Even as a baby, Cynthia was full of unpredictable humor and kept her parents laughing.

Joey fell in love with the baby, the only child she would have. The only child she would have to give away.

4

SIRENS

General MacArthur could see the Rock from his favorite balcony, which opened off the dining room. The jungle-covered island of Corregidor rose from the sea in the shape of a tadpole. At roughly one and a half miles wide and two and a half miles long, it was the largest of the four fortified islands planted in the mouth of Manila Bay, and it was divided into three defensive shelves: Topside, Middleside, and Bottomside, the low center of the island. Administrative offices were located Topside. Barracks and living quarters were on Middleside. And Bottomside held the cold storage installations, Filipino barracks, warehouses, the shop area, the power plant, and the docks. Beyond Bottomside rose Malinta Hill, reaching an elevation of four hundred feet above sea level. Inside the belly of the hill was an extensive tunnel system. A small landing field occupied the tail of the island, farther to the east.

If the United States and the underprepared Filipino army stood any chance of defending the islands, the Japanese could not be allowed access to Manila Harbor, and all that was protecting the harbor was Corregidor. The Rock would be the most important real estate in the archipelago.

Defense of the island fell to a Texan, Maj. Gen. George F. Moore, and he was in constant fear of a surprise attack before the Japanese declared war. He often stood Topside at night and peered out over the black water toward the lights of Manila. And every night, about a mile away from Corregidor, drifted a fleet of one hundred or more Japanese fishing boats, each one capable of carrying one hundred men. He thought about what might happen if the boats made a coordinated dash in the darkness for the island while his men were quietly sleeping.

For nearly the past year, Moore had been rushing to prepare the island for attack. He started by evacuating the families of American service personnel back to the United States. Then he doubled training time for the men involved with the harbor defense, subjecting them over and over to simulated Japanese attacks. He trained more radio operators and held practice air-raid tests. He ordered the construction of new barracks, new tunnels, and new roads, which snaked to nine new antiaircraft machine gun towers. He increased the number of men on twenty-four-hour alert. He leased an auxiliary mine planter, a ship called *Neptune*, and covered the Manila Bay passes with underwater mines.

In late November 1941, Moore received a message from MacArthur saying talks were breaking down with Japan and telling Moore to "take such measures as [you see] fit to insure the readiness of the command to meet any eventuality." Moore called his staff and ordered them to head for their battle stations. By the time the sun came up, they were as ready as they could be.

The surge of American weapons to the islands, the installation of new antiaircraft guns, and the fortification of Corregidor and Bataan, brought a sense of safety. People talked of the thousands of new planes parked on landing strips up and down the islands and of the brigade of tanks that regularly raced up and down the beaches. This was American military might on full display. It was hard to imagine Japan would attack.

★   ★   ★

Moore's phone rang at 3:40 AM on December 8. It was 8:40 AM on December 7 in Hawaii, more than five thousand miles away, on the other side of the International Date Line. The caller was manning the navy radio intercept installation on Corregidor. He told Moore he had just received two messages.

"Hostilities commenced with air raids on Pearl," he said.

"And the second?" Moore said.

"Air raids on Pearl Harbor. This is not drill."

Both had been signed by the naval commander in chief.

Moore sprang from his bed, dressed quickly, and hustled to the harbor defense command post, H Station, where his staff officers were gathering. He started rattling off orders. Alert the seaward defense commander, antiaircraft defense commander, and beach defense commander, he said. Tell them to ready sea and air surveillance against a surprise dawn attack. He told them to transmit the text of his orders to MacArthur at the headquarters of the US Army Forces in the Far East (USAFFE), in Manila. He suspended all passes and canceled the morning boat to Manila. He ordered the ordinance officer to establish munitions dumps and the surgeon to set up aid stations. He prepared them to put the war plan in place.

At 6:02 AM, a message came from USAFFE: "A state of war exists between the United States and Japan. Govern yourself accordingly."

The first air-raid siren blared at 10:26 AM when a flight of seventeen enemy bombers was spotted flying toward the island from the east. The fleet turned away before it was within range. But now there was no doubt.

5

SAFEGUARDS

First came the headaches, pounding and pulsing behind her temples, worming into the backs of her brown eyes, stealing her sleep.

Then came the fatigue, robbing her of energy and strength. She felt as though some force was slowly occupying her body, staking out its land under foreign flag. She kneeled and prayed with all the faith she could muster. She worried.

Then came the loss of appetite. For months she had to force herself to eat.

Then a small blemish appeared on her cheek, a pink splotch on her light skin that first could have been mistaken for a pimple or a bug bite of some sort but soon began to take an odd shape, spreading, swelling outward, expanding, an amorphous alien growth that could not be dislodged.

She finally told Renato.

He took her to the best infectious disease specialist he knew, and the doctor ran a battery of tests and delivered the diagnosis, which fell out of his mouth like a stone. Leprosy.

She struggled to understand what it meant, seized by confusion, her future tumbling, crashing. She felt betrayed by her body. The scriptures crawled through her mind, Leviticus, Deuteronomy, 1 and 2 Kings, the Gospels.

And if the priest see that, behold, the scab spreadeth in the skin, then the priest shall pronounce him unclean (Leviticus 13:8).

The leprosy therefore of Naaman shall cleave unto thee, and unto thy seed for ever (2 Kings 5:27).

She pictured the worst, the loss of feeling, the crooking of her fingers and toes, the boils upon her face and arms and back. Renato tried to calm her, to inform her that the stigma was incorrect and her false ideas of biblical leprosy were not factually sound. He told her that it wasn't as contagious as many other diseases and explained to her the known phases and treatments. He put his arm around her.

"We will live through this," he said.

"At least there are medicines," she said. "The disease can be cured."

"True," Renato said. "With the proper rest and medicines."

Nonetheless, she would be judged. Too little was known about the disease. In Manila, lepers were feared, were made to ring a bell and carry a sign indicating they were contagious. Those who complied were shunned, dispatched to live outside the city in colonies. There were some eight thousand leprosy victims being treated at that time in the Philippines, with primitive medicines like chaulmoogra oil and its derivatives, but no one knew how many were in hiding or wandering among the general population.

The doctor informed the young couple that to safeguard Cynthia, who was just five years old, from infection, she and Joey could not live under the same roof.

Joey died a thousand deaths.

The pain was excruciating. She called it her Calvary. She knew what she had to do. She couldn't even kiss her daughter good-bye.

Cynthia went to live with Rene's mother, a frugal Spanish woman who loved her granddaughter. Rene moved in with his mother as well, leaving Joey alone in their Florida Street home, with two servant girls. Joey took pains to be careful. She made certain everything she used and sent out of the house had been sterilized.

Rene found a doctor who would treat Joey in private, in her home, and the treatments seemed to be working. The skin lesions were kept at bay. The fatigue and headaches were bearable. She maintained her beauty, and though she didn't venture out but to receive Mass, she maintained her status in society.

Nobody seemed to notice anything amiss. She and Rene and the servant girls and the doctor had a simple secret they'd share with no one.

6

BOMBS

The newsboys shouted from the corners of Makati and Ermita and Intramuros, their voices rising above the Filipinos in their finest clothes queuing before cathedral doors for the most important Mass of the year.

"Honolulu bombed!" the boys hollered, shaking pages in their inky hands.

The faithful were going down on their knees as word spread that it wasn't just Honolulu. High overhead, Mitsubishi G4Ms adorned with blood-red suns let loose explosives over territory that had belonged to the United States since the 1898 Treaty of Paris—Clark Field to the northwest, Baguio to the north, Iba to the east, Del Carmen to the southeast—catching fleets of US airplanes, P-40s and P-35As and B-17s, on the ground, immobile, the jet fuel igniting and giving rise for the last time to flaming fuselages.

Doors blew off hinges. Nipa huts disintegrated. Black sprays of sand climbed over the treetops. Flames sprinted across tarmac. The detonations came quick and cracked like short, sharp thunder, and towers of fire licked at the sky, then gave way to pillars of black smoke. The piers were burning. The docks were burning. Depots and hangars jumped from the earth and separated at the seams, and wafts of cordite filtered through the trees. The sky was a horde of white hornets. American soldiers, boots planted on shaking ground, fired .45-caliber pistols worthlessly into the air. The few planes that were scrambled came down as quickly as they had gone up. Guns lit up on Corregidor as enemy bombers passed to the east, out of range. Fire leaped across rice paddies and parade grounds and city streets. The Twenty-Sixth Cavalry, the last horse unit in the American army, the most professional and best-trained combat unit in the islands, advanced in long columns down Dewey Boulevard, northbound, their mounts rustling nervously in trailers with each new concussion, a prideful portrait of an impoverished strategy.

The twelve-acre campus of the Ateneo de Manila was covered in festive bunting, and a band played in the schoolyard as the boys, out of class for the feast, gathered for Mass at noon in a state of confusion. *Was it true?* The American Jesuit fathers were searching for information themselves about the attacks outside the city.

"I've just been informed that Fort Stotsenberg has been bombed," the rector told the boys, interrupting Mass, "and that the United States has declared war on Japan."

Father Forbes Monaghan saw a newsboy run into the Ateneo with the morning paper as a throng gathered around. "State of war!" the boy shouted.

Planes soon appeared over Manila, but the boys on the ground had trouble believing they were Japanese planes. The Japanese didn't even make good toys, they thought. How could they build airplanes that could reach Manila? Some believed they were German planes being flown by German pilots. All day they came, whoever they were, and even though the city was under a forced blackout that night, the planes still roared in. The pilots used the shorelines of the Pasig River and Manila Bay as navigational tools and struck Nichols Field, just to the southeast of the city, and the Cavite naval base on Manila Bay. Maj. Gen. George Moore and the soldiers on Corregidor watched Cavite burn.

When the sun came up, Father Monaghan watched the sky as thirty pursuit planes raced north to repel another attack on Clark Field. It was the first and last time he'd see them as a fighting organization. The next day, they were gone, just like the bomber fleets.

US president Franklin Delano Roosevelt told the world what he knew, that the Empire of Japan had suddenly and deliberately attacked the United States at Hawaii, which was just one piece of a wild and surprising portrait of the Asian nation's march across the Pacific. Yesterday they attacked Malaya, he said.

Last night, Hong Kong.

Last night, Guam.

Last night, the Philippine Islands.

Last night, Wake Island.

This morning, Midway Island.

"As commander-in-chief of the army and navy," he said, "I have directed that all measures be taken for our defense. But always will our whole nation remember the character of the onslaught against us. No matter how long it may take us to overcome this premeditated invasion, the American people in their righteous might will win through to absolute victory."

Quickly, the Philippine government activated reserve divisions, and young Filipino soldiers began to report to the University of Santo Tomas, on España Boulevard, the second-oldest university outside of Europe. They marched in prepared for the unknown, cured of their sentiments, ready to defend a country that was home but that they had never really owned. Some had barely a week of training; the veterans had no more than four months. The police commandeered private trucks and buses across the metropolis, and the long columns of transports carrying soldiers by the hundreds pushed north out of Santo Tomas toward Lingayen Gulf, the most likely landing shore for Japanese foot soldiers. The army moving out of the city had been organized just four years before. The men were raw, inexperienced, and ill equipped. They came out of the rice paddies and out of merchant tents and off fishing boats and didn't fully understand why they were fighting for America. But they were vicious and loyal.

They trusted the Americans. They trusted MacArthur. As Japanese bombers pounded their shores, sinking their boats in the harbor, blasting their buildings in Pasay and Malate, they cinched their belts and tugged on their cheap US-issued shoes and fired unfamiliar Enfield rifles into the sky. Even those not in uniform trusted. As Japanese troops steamed toward landing zones on Luzon, they insulted the enemy in the pages of the *Manila Herald* and on radio stations like KZRH, where Leon Maria Guerrero of the Ermita Guerreros, who had learned to use the equipment with the Ateneo Jesuits, started the *Victory Broadcast*.

At the Ateneo, telegrams poured in from frightened parents telling their children to come home. Some packed up quickly and left with short good-byes. The Jesuit fathers decided to send the boarders home, all but the ROTC cadets. Word reached the Ateneo that General MacArthur and Philippine president Manuel Quezon had instructed the cadets who had finished the basic ROTC training to stay on, to be rapidly trained for military service and sent to the field as officers when training ended in January. Hundreds of boys stayed and began drilling, digging trenches with intensity, and studying war plans.

The boarders who hadn't left, plus those from closed schools across the city, grabbed their belongings and rushed to the pier to catch one of the few interisland boats leaving Manila to return home to their families in other island provinces, Cebu and Davao and Zamboanga and Mindanao. Some twelve hundred crammed onto the *Corregidor*, an eighteen-ton transport ship that was fleeing Manila harbor for the safety of the outlying islands. But the ship struck a mine at the mouth of Manila Bay and sank in two minutes. Navy small boats picked up 280 oil-covered survivors, and others helped as well, searching for the living in shark-infested waters, but some 500 passengers were lost. Those who survived were taken to a building at the Ateneo that had been turned into a Red Cross station. The Jesuits accepted any survivors, and the campus—with its main academic building, the famous Manila Observatory, the auditorium, the laboratories, the library, the chapel, and the gymnasium—became an unofficial refugee center. When word spread that the religious school was taking refugees, more began to arrive. The population swelled by an additional four hundred people, from the navy yard at Cavite and Nichols Field, women without husbands and babies without fathers.

The days ticked by, and the bombs fell like clockwork on the airfield in Zambales Province, on Fort Wint, on Cabcaban airfield on Bataan.

On December 22, Maj. Gen. George Moore, holding the fort on Corregidor, received word that the enemy was near. Japan had made landings to the north and south, and foot soldiers were pushing southward in the central plain of Luzon toward Manila.

On December 23, an army officer told an assembly of ROTC boys at the Ateneo that they were to go home, to help their families and save themselves. En masse the boys objected, begging to be allowed to go to the front and fight as a united battalion. But the officer insisted, and slowly, grudgingly, the boys dispersed. Their day was to come, fighting as guerrillas in the hills and city streets, but many cried in that somber moment.

On the morning of Christmas Eve, Moore learned that MacArthur and his family, USAFFE headquarters staff, and Philippine president Manuel Quezon and his family would all be on Corregidor by nightfall. The newspapers and radio stations were declaring Manila an "open city," suggesting US and Filipino troops would not try to defend it against attack. The Filipinos wondered what had happened to their great American military leader.

If this wasn't retreat, what was it?

The commander-in-chief of the Imperial Japanese Expeditionary Forces to the Philippines would issue the first of several draconian warnings, sending fear pulsing through Filipino society.

Notice

1. The Japanese Armed Forces wishes to share the well-beings with the officials and people of the native land.

    Wait the arrivals of the Japanese troops with confidence and ease. Regardless of the nationality, no one is necessary to flee.

2. Making resistance or taking the hostile actions against the Japanese Armed Forces, in any manner, leads the whole native land into the ashes. Therefore everyone should come under the protection of the Japanese Armed Forces without seeing even one drop of blood, and should continue daily business as usual.

3. Anyone who falls under the any of the followings will be considered as the interfering of the well-beings of the native peoples, and therefore be subject to the death penalty. Be aware of not commiting any of said crime.

   (1) Those who show hostility against the Japanese Armed Forces.

   (2) Those who jeopardize or break any existing means in politics, economics, industry, transportation, communication, financials, and etc.

   (3) Those who disturb the thoughts of the officials and peoples.

   (4) Any actions disturbing the economic and financial status.

Those who report to the Japanese Forces any flagrant offence or preventing of any said crime will be rewarded by the Japanese Armed Forces.

COMMANDER-IN-CHIEF

THE JAPANESE ARMED FORCE

7

ENVELOPE

The woman in the black dress called out to the young priest as he strolled around the Ateneo de Manila compound. He turned to see a diminished human being, her head and arms covered by a veil. She waved. He waved back and kept walking.

She called out once more, and he spun around. He'd given his last peso to a beggar at the Ateneo gates the day before, and there was little hope of getting any more. He hesitated. She beckoned him to come closer. When he did, he could see that the veil covered open sores on her arms, face, and legs.

"Are you Padre Hulian?" she asked.

"I'm Father Fred Julien," he replied. "Possibly you are looking for a Jesuit priest of the same or a similar name."

Father Julien hadn't been in Manila long, certainly not long enough to be recognized on the street. He wasn't supposed to be in the Philippines. Newly ordained, he had taken a train from his hometown of Albany, New York, across the country to San Francisco, and then boarded the SS *President Grant*, bound for Burma, where his band of La Salette fathers were starting a mission. They'd brought along six packing crates full of provisions—enough, they hoped, to last ten years in Burma. But the fathers noticed something strange after a short stop in Hawaii. The *Grant* was suddenly part of a five-ship convoy that was entirely blacked out at night, and a spotter plane came and went from a cruiser escort each day. Close to Guam, the entire convoy made a sharp turn for Manila, where it arrived on December 7, which was December 6 in Hawaii. The next day, after Father Julien said Mass, the captain of the *Grant* announced that Pearl Harbor had been bombed. He told his passengers to sleep ashore in Manila that night because the Japanese might try to bomb the ships in the harbor. He told them the *Grant* would leave for Australia the next morning. If only. The La Salette fathers left their luggage and provisions aboard the ship and went in search of a place to stay at one of Manila's religious communities. The Jesuit priests at Ateneo de Manila, six blocks from the piers, invited them to stay. The students had been sent home when war broke out, so there were plenty of beds. But when the fathers returned to the pier the next morning, the *Grant* was gone, along with their luggage and provisions and a four-hundred-pound church bell for the mission in Burma. What little money the fathers had they soon handed over to the Jesuits at the Ateneo for room and board. Father Julien was very aware that he was penniless and stuck in a foreign country now engaged in war.

The mysterious lady in black asked him once more if he was Padre Hulian, a La Salette priest.

"Are not there three of you stranded in my country?" she asked.

"That is correct," Father Julien answered.

She reached inside the folds of her dress and fished out an envelope and handed it to the priest. She told him that someone had asked her to give it to him. Then she turned and walked away.

Father Julien opened the envelope and gasped. He counted the money. One hundred pesos.

He began asking the Jesuits about the lady in black. One of them told him her name. Josefina Guerrero. He'd see her again.

8

BOYS

The convoy entered Lingayen Gulf after nightfall on December 22—eighty Japanese ships carrying Lt. Gen. Masaharu Homma and his Fourteenth Army of forty-three thousand soldiers who disembarked and fought ashore. The only challenge to the massive fleet was from a few 155-millimeter guns. On land, it quickly seemed like they knew exactly what they were doing. More and more it seemed as though the enemy had been living among the unsuspecting Filipinos, watching, waiting. The Japanese fishing fleets, friendly before the outbreak, knew every landing. The kindly Japanese photographer, who owned a legitimate business, had been taking pictures of the rapidly built fortifications. The laborers and farmers and merchants, it would be learned, were part of a patchwork of thousands of spies who for years had been turning over information to the empire in preparation for this day of conquest.

Maybe if the Filipino fighters were better trained or weren't fighting with World War I–era rifles, they could have driven back the attacking force. There was no choice but to retreat, lest they be easily overrun and slaughtered. And when Japanese troops landed at Lamon Bay on the east coast of Luzon, forty miles south of Manila, General MacArthur saw a nightmare coming: two forces working toward each other like the jaws of a "great military pincer," he later wrote.

MacArthur was shocked, according to those around him. He was unable to give commands to his staff officers. When he finally got his bearings, he ordered troops from all over South Luzon to withdraw to Bataan, where the US and Philippine soldiers would make a final stand, side by side. They streamed through Manila, saying good-bye and "It'll be a long time before you see us again," then rushed toward the peninsula, calling home one last time along the way, blowing up bridges behind them. He ordered the units fighting the Japanese in the north to "stand and fight, slip back and dynamite," a delay-action retrograde maneuver that would give troops from the south time to get to Bataan.

The ROTC boys from the Ateneo and cadets from the Philippine Military Academy—the young ones who weren't commissioned but refused to go home—began trying to organize. They wanted to fight. They wanted to go to Bataan. There were about forty-three boys from the Ateneo alone, and they joined together with the military academy cadets and University of Santo Tomas students who couldn't return to their home islands, forming what they called the Second Regular Division. Some of them were fourteen and fifteen years old. Their elders were nineteen. They had courage but no weapons. They went to the Ateneo, to the Jesuit fathers, and asked if they could use the ROTC weapons.

"If you have authority, we will give you the guns," one of the fathers said. "Anyway, if the Japanese get these, they'll use them against us."

Father Monaghan, who had taught many of the boys, felt the two-way pull of pity and pride. They were all so eager, and so naive.

"Wherever you are, know that back here we will be praying for you every day," he told them.

"Yes, father," one said. "We know you will."

And with that, a bunch of Catholic boys who had lied about their ages, who had left notes informing their mothers and fathers, boarded buses with rifles on their shoulders and began the long trip to Bataan to fight. As they left Manila, some of the boys began to cry. They were men enough to go to war, but they wept openly as their city burned in a blur outside the window.

The Japanese warplanes continued screaming overhead, shelling the riverfront district and Intramuros, despite the surrender of the beautiful city. Convents and colleges erupted into rubble. Turned-up ships dotted the bay like tombstones. Knives of black smoke stabbed skyward. Everything burned. The piers, the oil depots of Pandacan, the port area. Those who could fled for the countryside. Those who couldn't stayed inside, doors locked. The areas not blazing were deserted, empty black curtains drawn over the windows.

When the sun slid down and the sky turned red, the casualties of the day's raids began to arrive at the Ateneo, a trickle at first, then a flood. Father Monaghan saw men running and an ambulance with a busted windshield trailing behind them. He ran to help the driver, who jumped out and threw open the rear doors. Inside lay the wounded, covered in blood. Some were naked, for their clothing had been blown clean off their bodies. When the fathers had emptied the ambulance, the driver shouted, "The port area is filled with others like these and no one is there to pick them up."

"Let's go," Monaghan told him, climbing in.

They raced to the Bureau of Printing, near the port, a temporary shelter that had taken a direct hit and was now ablaze. The priest found a pile of bodies at the door and a fire raging beyond. He snatched his sacred oils from his pocket and began anointing the dead.

Placards rose in a place now shocked by abandonment. OPEN CITY, the signs over Taft and Rizal Avenues declared. Manila's gates were wide. The feared "yellow menace" would arrive any day. The men of Manila wondered how they'd be treated. The thought of how their wives and daughters would be treated brought them to tears. There were already whispers of the Rape of Nanking, in which brutal Japanese troops massacred and raped as many as three hundred thousand noncombatants during the country's war with China. What would happen to the citizens of Manila?

Looting broke out at the piers first, then moved uptown to the grocery stores. Anything of value—bread, sugar, rice, cracked wheat—disappeared from shelves. Pharmacies were hit, too, and medicine grew scarce.

Carlos Romulo, a colonel on MacArthur's staff, had been left behind to see that all of the headquarters' personnel made the move to Corregidor. On New Year's Eve, he drove down Dewey Boulevard to say good-bye to his wife, then headed for the pier to catch a boat for Corregidor. He stopped at the Manila Hotel, where MacArthur had enjoyed the penthouse in peacetime. As the city outside burned, a band played in the lobby and well-dressed guests slow danced into the last American morning.

9

HOBNAILED BOOTS

The first sound they heard in Manila was a chorus of hobnailed boots on stone like some sort of faint hymn carried on the January wind, getting closer, closer. The Japanese soldiers had moved so quickly on the city that the rumor spread that they'd been seen swinging limb to limb through the jungle like monkeys. There was no challenge when they arrived at the ancient city.

Manila had a new regime by January 3, 1942.

Around the city the Japanese soldiers marched, rounding up some five thousand British and American civilians, then the Dutch, Australians, and Canadians, pulling them from their homes and businesses and shuffling them off to Rizal Stadium, where they were sorted and sent to the harsh Bilibid Prison or the University of Santo Tomas, which was quickly converted into a prison camp and filled to capacity with men, women, and children. Fear caught in the throats of wives stripped from husbands, children snatched from mothers.

On January 4, soldiers showed up at the Ateneo to round up American civilians for internment. The priests were told to pack their bags because they were next. Businessmen who saw what was coming had opened up their warehouses and invited citizens to take what they could before the Japanese did. The Jesuits, sensing the war could last a long while, claimed wine in barrels and all the flour they could carry so Mass could be administered daily. And it did go on as planned, but it was rationed from the first day. Priests prepared a small host and put wine into the chalice with an eyedropper.

Confusion reigned in those early days, exacerbated by a curious custom among the Japanese soldiers that drove the Filipinos mad. It was common practice for the soldiers to slap citizens who wouldn't or couldn't follow directions or didn't show proper respect. If a Filipino did not bow to a Japanese soldier, or did not bow low enough for his satisfaction, the citizen could expect a hard slap across the face. What was customary in Japan was incredibly insulting to the Filipinos. And while Japanese propaganda posters were being plastered across the city, promising they came as friends to assist the

Asiatic people, assaults on citizens solidified Philippine loyalty to America.

Alejandro Roces, a young man educated at the Ateneo, saw his fellow countrymen beaten in the streets, their hands tied behind their backs, chained to posts. He felt as though the Japanese were trying to break the spirits of Filipinos. Rather than growing scared, anger prompted Roces to join the resistance. Gustavo Ingles witnessed Japanese soldiers drive through his hometown, and when they saw young girls, stop the trucks and chase the girls down. The first-year Philippine Military Academy cadet was hurt and sad. The soldiers thought they could take whatever they wanted. Ingles felt he had to do something, so he began conspiring with his friends in San Juan. *What are we going to do about this?*

10

BASTARDS

The boys on Bataan surged and retreated, advanced and fell back, making the enemy earn every square inch of the hellish Florida-shaped peninsula, every cliff and mangled banyan tree, every bamboo thicket and tangle of wait-a-minute vines. They lost weight and sleep and caught malaria, dengue fever, hookworm, and beriberi, which caused the men to vomit and slur their speech and made their eyes flick around in their heads unnaturally. They carried guns that failed to fire and grenades that did not explode and letters that began "Dear Mama." They heard regularly that a mile-long convoy of supplies was steaming toward the island, that B-17s and P-40s would soon appear in the sky, that relief was coming. General MacArthur was party to the lie, though he was unaware of it. He crossed to the peninsula from Corregidor to help boost morale. He talked to the rawboned Gen. Jonathan Wainwright and his junior officers and toured the peninsula, talking to his boys, encouraging them to keep up the fight.

"Help is definitely on the way," he told the ragged soldiers. "We must hold out until it comes."

It did not come, not that day nor any day thereafter. There were now more than one hundred thousand soldiers and civilians crowded onto Bataan, and supplies were lower than ever. The men kept fighting, though, and through gritted teeth they sang made-up songs that captured the dire frustration of their lost cause:

We're the battling bastards of Bataan:
No mama, no papa, no Uncle Sam,
No aunts, no uncles, no nephews, no nieces,
No rifles, no planes, or artillery pieces,
And nobody gives a damn.

The simple fact that the men had held off Japan from con-
quering the peninsula as December turned to January and January
encroached on February, despite the empire's continuous supply
of fresh troops and despite the fact that the Filipino soldiers were
wearing coconut hulls for helmets, was noteworthy. Bataan was virtually the only spot in the Pacific where Japanese advancement had
been stymied. They had found success everywhere else they had
invaded: Singapore, Burma, Siam, Sumatra, Borneo, Wake, Guam,
the Bismarks, the Gilberts. War planners knew Australia would be
next. Japanese bombers had already made runs against the key port
of Darwin. In less than two months, the Japanese Empire had grown
to cover almost a seventh of the globe. The only real resistance was
on the Bataan Peninsula, where American and Filipino troops had
dug in to fight.

Henry Stimson, the US secretary of war, told Philippines president Manuel Quezon, "Your gallant defense is thrilling the American people. As soon as our power is organized we shall come in
force and drive the invader from your soil."

In the middle of December, Maj. Gen. George Moore, still on
Corregidor, learned that Germany and Italy had also declared war
on the United States, and each day that ticked past brought news
that suggested the Axis powers, advancing across Europe and Africa
and now the Pacific, had the war in hand.

But by the end of the month, most of the US and Filipino forces
had retreated to Bataan, and they were proving hard to dislodge. "A
final stand," is what Moore called it.

President Roosevelt promised the full support of the United
States in a special address to the people of the Philippines on
December 28, 1941. He cabled Manuel Quezon after. "The peo-

ple of the United States will never forget what the people of the
Philippines are doing these days and will do in the days to come,"
he wrote. "I give to the people of the Philippines my solemn pledge
that their freedom will be retained and their independence established and redeemed. The entire resources in men and materials of
the United States stands behind that pledge."

On December 29, just before noon, Japan rocked the fortified
Corregidor in its first aerial attack, with eighty-one medium bombers and ten dive-bombers dropping three-hundred-pound bombs.
There were no friendly planes in the air, and there wouldn't be for
the entire operation.

The medium bombers came first in formations of twenty-seven;
then those broke into three formations of nine planes each, all of
them below twenty thousand feet, crossing the island lengthwise.
The first bombs fell on the hospital, the antiaircraft gun batteries,
the officers' club, the Topside and Middleside barracks, the Topside
water tank, the officers' quarters, the garage, ships in Corregidor
Bay, and the navy gasoline storage dump at the tail of the island.
Fires broke out as wooden structures and gas depots burst toward
the sky. Power went out. Communication lines were disrupted. The
antiaircraft firing batteries on the islands thwacked all afternoon,
bringing down thirteen enemy planes, until the bombers nosed up
to higher altitudes, outside of the guns' reach. The smaller strafing
planes followed the bombers, hammering the antiaircraft gun batteries. Twenty men were killed and eighty wounded.

The following afternoon, outside the east portal to Malinta Tunnel, Manuel Quezon was sworn in as the first president of the new
Philippine Commonwealth. In his short inaugural address, he spoke
of air raids and of bombs falling on women and children and of
Japan's superiority on air, land, and sea. Then he called for unity in
the new fight.

"To all Americans in the Philippines, soldiers and civilians alike,
I want to say that our common ordeal has fused our hearts in a
single purpose and an everlasting affection," he said. "My fellow

countrymen, this is the most momentous period of our history. As we face the grim realities of war, let us rededicate ourselves to the great principles of freedom and democracy for which our forefathers fought and died. The present war is being fought for these same principles."

Following the ceremony, the Ninety-First Coast Artillery Band was to play the national anthems of the United States and the Philippines, but their barracks had been bombed and their instruments were burned.

11

VOLUNTEER

Her body was failing, and she was scared. So little was known about her affliction, and the void was filled with terror.

Though her husband's main interest was infectious diseases, he knew far more about tuberculosis, which caused some thirty thousand deaths a year in the islands, than leprosy. *Mycobacterium leprae* was among the first bacilli identified, back in 1873, but it remained a medical mystery. It wasn't part of the standard medical school curriculum, and few physicians bothered to learn about it. There was no vaccine for leprosy, and no one could say for sure whether it was hereditary or a contagious disease. It was commonly believed that you got leprosy by sharing food or drink with a leper or by touching an infected person.

In the Philippines, leprosy sufferers hid the early symptoms under clothing as long as possible, until it was no longer an option. When the lesions couldn't be covered, victims were ejected from their communities, becoming charity cases, outcasts, or beggars, forced to leave behind their lives, their jobs, their loved ones. Because of unfortunate wording in the Old Testament, leprosy was regarded in some cultures as a punishment for sinfulness, transforming sufferers' physical ailments into a moral condition. Stigmatized, they were driven into hellish government- or church-run colonies in the rural provinces, away from society.

There were some eight thousand known cases in the islands at the start of the war, but the chaos of battle had sent many more into hiding for fear they'd become the easiest casualties of the new occupying regime. This was not an irrational fear. In 1912, soldiers in a city in southern China rounded up lepers in their own colony, drove them to a pit, and shot them, women and children included. And then they burned the bodies. Fifty-three people died that day, and the massacre was met with public approval. More recently, in 1937, in the Chinese province of Guangdong, leprosy victims were promised an allowance of ten cents—a ruse—and when they gathered to accept the allotment, more than fifty of them were executed.

The American health authorities in the Pacific Islands adopted a policy of segregation and isolation, shipping the afflicted to far-flung colonies or medical facilities for treatment with an injectable form of chaulmoogra oil, the only drug that showed any promise. With the outbreak of war between Japan and the United States, those who weren't caught and dispatched to leper colonies were now stuck in cities with shuttered pharmacies.

Joey desperately needed medicine to keep her disease under control, but it was virtually impossible to get in the shredded city. Sometimes the drugs could be found on the black market, but the expense was so high, out of reach. So the leprosy ran rampant, attacking her body, destroying her flesh, and causing her joints to stiffen.

She couldn't just stay at home, in isolation, and waste away. She prayed, sought higher instruction, until one day she had an epiphany. If she believed anything, it was that even the lowliest could be a vessel, could be of service to the greater good. She thought about Joan of Arc, the peasant girl who led France into battle, driving back the English and reclaiming the crown. If she was going to die, she would do so with dignity, face her fate with honor.

In the face of slow death, she decided to live, to use whatever was left to help her people. She approached a friend she knew to be in the underground resistance movement that had formed since

Japanese soldiers marched into the city on January 2, 1942. The network was vast, but the guerrillas lived in constant fear. The Japanese army was attempting to purge the city of guerrillas. Soldiers would cordon off a neighborhood, called a *zona*, and position sentries at every possible entry or exit. They would then call all residents out of their homes and force them to parade past a mole, a Filipino traitor wearing a burlap sack over his head. Known as the "secret eye," the traitor would indicate with a nod or gesture when a suspected guerrilla passed. The soldiers then pulled that person from the line for questioning. Most never returned home.

Joey knew the risks. Still, she volunteered.

"I want to be a good soldier," she told her friend.

"Then go underground," he said. "I will give you a name."

Her friend gave her the name of a man she knew well from the Ateneo. She was surprised to learn that he was a leader in the underground resistance. She was due for a lot of surprises. She tracked the man down and told him she wanted to work for the resistance.

"We don't take children," he told her. She was only twenty-four.

"You'd be surprised what children can do," she told him. "After all, Joan of Arc was just a young girl—not much more than a child—wasn't she?"

12

LEAFLETS

The bombers appeared again, three of them on January 26, and the sirens shouted, but there were no concussions to follow, not this time.

Leaflets fluttered down from the sky like wounded birds, spinning and somersaulting in the morning light, catching in the treetops and tumbling to the dirt. They fell over Corregidor and Caballe, El Fraile and Carabao and Bataan, into ravines and onto rooftops and at the feet of soldiers, tired and hungry and homesick.

On one side, a picture of a nude brunette sexily seated, her left hand in her hair, her face and breasts bathed in studio light. On the other was a note:

TICKET TO ARMISTICE
USE THIS TICKET, SAVE YOUR LIFE
YOU WILL BE KINDLY TREATED
FOLLOW THESE INSTRUCTIONS
1. Come towards our lines waving a white flag.
2. Strap your gun over your left shoulder muzzle down and pointed behind you.
3. Show this ticket to the sentry.
4. Any number of you may surrender with this one ticket.
JAPANESE ARMY HEADQUARTERS

13

GONE

The general was prepared to die.

By all accounts, MacArthur had been unafraid to stand outside Malinta Tunnel, unflinching, without so much as a helmet, as Japanese bombers pounded the Rock into dust and ash. They didn't talk about defeat on Corregidor, but without the supplies and reinforcements Washington had promised, the men on Bataan stood no chance. Nor did the men on Corregidor. A colonel under MacArthur broached the subject, suggesting maybe Roosevelt had been bluffing about the support convoy to get MacArthur and his men to hold out as long as possible, to delay the Japanese advance south and essentially allow the United States time to protect Australia.

"If you are correct," MacArthur told him, "then never in history was so large and gallant an army written off so callously!"

MacArthur was a brave son of a bitch, and he faced the reality that he might die upon Corregidor. He tried to send his wife, Jean, and young son to safety on a submarine or with the Quezon family, which was preparing a daring escape through enemy waters to Australia, but Jean would have none of it. "Jean is my first soldier," the general told an aide. Another asked about his son. "He is a soldier's son," MacArthur said.

As the days ticked by, President Roosevelt had second thoughts about leaving the new war's only hero to die unprotected. Getting him out alive would be a huge challenge. He kept his thoughts private.

MacArthur said good-bye to his friend Manuel Quezon, who was boarding a submarine called the *Swordfish* for Australia. The Philippines' first president gave MacArthur his ring. "When they find your body," he said, "I want them to know that you fought for my country."

On February 23, MacArthur's orders came from the commander in chief. He was directed to a southern island to assess whether a Bataan defense could be sustained. But then he was to go to Melbourne to take command of all US troops. MacArthur wrestled with his decision for days. At a staff meeting in Malinta Tunnel, he told his comrades he'd made a decision. He was going to refuse the president's orders, give up his position, and join the troops fighting on Bataan as a volunteer, but he acquiesced after his staff protested. He told Gen. Jonathan Wainright to tell his men on Bataan that he had protested many times but had to follow orders. "If I get through to Australia you know I'll come back as soon as I can with as much as I can," the general said.

"I'll be on Bataan if I'm alive," Wainright replied.

On March 6, a Filipino gave Harbor Defense Headquarters a message sent by the Japanese. "Our invincible artillery will pound Corregidor into submission, batter it, weaken it," the message said, "preparatory to a final assault by crack Japanese landing troops. Be wise, surrender now and receive preferential Japanese treatment." But the skies were quiet on March 7, 8, 9, and 10.

As he prepared to leave the island, MacArthur told Maj. Gen. George Moore to reduce rations on Corregidor to last four months, until June 1942. He cautioned Moore that in case of the ultimate fall of Corregidor, Moore was to make sure that the armament was destroyed to such an extent that it could not be used against an American effort to recapture the Philippines.

On March 11, after dark, General MacArthur, along with his wife, son, and staff, headed to the pier, where four patrol torpedo boats idled, waiting to whisk them south to Mindanao, where a bomber would fly them to Melbourne.

MacArthur clasped Moore's hand in a fervent embrace and a tear fell down his cheek.

"Don't give up the fort, George," he said. "I'll be back."

The general, dressed in civilian clothes, took one last look at the bombed-to-hell island, then replaced his cap and climbed aboard. Under a moonless sky, they motored south. MacArthur was headed toward his future, toward "Supreme Command of the whole Southwest Pacific," as Roosevelt would put it. But the general had left his men behind.

14

ESPIONAGE

Joey lived near a building that had been converted into a Japanese garrison. Her first assignment was to watch the garrison and report all troop movements in and out. Her friends were afraid she was being reckless.

"If I don't run risks, I won't find out anything worthwhile," she told them. "All the important things are carefully watched."

She hid behind the shutters in the windows of her house, scratching notes on a piece of paper. She counted the trucks and the soldiers in the beds of the trucks, noting their appearance, whether their uniforms were soiled or clean when they returned. She noted the men who entered the garrison, what time, when they left, and in which direction. When she had filled a notebook, she hid it and carried it to the address she had been given and handed it to a suspicious-looking man. She gave him her underground name: Billy Ferrer. He thanked her and closed the door.

Not long after that, some clueless Japanese officers living near her home invited her to a party at the Engineering Building. The thought of going was revolting, but she realized it could be an opportunity to get information. The Japanese had been busy fortifying the university campus, and she wanted to know what, specifically, they were doing. She asked two friends to accompany her, and once on campus, she nonchalantly asked for a tour of the buildings. The hosts agreed. Joey was full of endless questions.

"Why does that woman ask so many questions?" one of the officers asked.

Her friends were worried about the suspicion.

"Did you hear that officer," one said. "Look out."

Joey assumed a new tact: flighty ignorance. She started asking silly questions to throw them off. After a few minutes, she noticed a large entrance dug into the ground behind the Engineering Building and saw soldiers going in and out.

"What is that?" she asked.

"That is an air-raid shelter," the officer said.

"May we go inside?" Joey asked.

"There is nothing inside worth looking at," the man said.

The tour continued until Joey again noticed a similar opening near the corner of Isaac Peral Street and Taft Avenue and again asked what it was.

"That is another air-raid shelter," the man said.

She watched a man walk out of the hole and recognized him. She had seen the same man entering the hole behind the Engineering Building. These weren't air-raid shelters; it was one long, secret tunnel. That evening she drew the tunnel on a map.

15

SPEEDO

More leaflets fell over Bataan as the men, down to three-eighths rations, wasted away, dropping weight and dropping dead in the sand, from bullets or beriberi. They fell like a blizzard of white-winged butterflies.

"Your U.S. Convoy is due in the Philippines on April 15th but you won't be alive to see it. Ha! Ha!"

The soldiers used the leaflets as toilet paper.

Still, they fought, as Japanese soldiers pushed them into a smaller and smaller area. Four-fifths of them struggled with malaria, and three-quarters had dysentery. A third of the soldiers suffered from beriberi. The boys joked that God had seen fit to create two kinds of mosquitoes for the Philippines: the big ones that bit in the daytime and caused dengue fever and the small ones that bit you at night and gave you malaria.

The rations were down to fifteen ounces per man per day, and half of that was rice. Digging a foxhole, which typically took an hour, now took all day. The two open-air hospitals were stuffed with ten thousand men, and seven hundred more men came down with malaria every day. The grunts were so starved that the decision was made to butcher the Twenty-Sixth Cavalry's horses, the same beasts that had led the charge at the village of Marong, the last mounted cavalry charge in US military history. The horses were the first real meat the soldiers had eaten in weeks.

One Thursday afternoon in the middle of March, Japanese planes dropped thousands of beer cans on Bataan. They were empty but for a letter.

> To His Excellency Major-General Jonathon Wain-wright, Commander-in-Chief of the United States in the Philippines.
>
> We have the honor to address you in accordance with the humanitarian principles of "Bushido," the code of the Japanese warrior.
>
> It will be recalled that, some time ago, a note advising honorable surrender was sent to the Commander-in-Chief of your fighting forces. To this, no reply, as yet, has been received. . . .
>
> Your Excellency, you have fought to the best of your ability. What dishonor is there in avoiding needless bloodshed? What disgrace is there in following the defenders of Hong Kong, Singapore, and the Netherlands East Indies in the acceptance of honorable defeat? Your Excellency, your duty has been performed. Accept our sincere advice and save the lives of those officers and men under your command. The International Law will be strictly adhered to by the Imperial Japanese Forces and Your Excellency and those under your command will be treated accordingly. The joy and happiness of those whose lives will be saved and the delight and relief of their dear ones and families would be beyond the expression of words. We call upon you to reconsider this proposition with due thought.
>
> If a reply to this advisory note is not received from Your Excellency through a special messenger by noon of

March 22nd, 1942, we shall consider ourselves at liberty
to take any action whatsoever.

The letters were signed by General Homma. When Wainwright
read it, he said, "The bastards could at least have sent a few full cans
of beer."

As April neared, the soldiers were urged to write their last letters to loved ones. They were also asked if they wished to take out
$10,000 life insurance policies. Wainwright ordered radio opera-
tions to cease so they could transmit thirty thousand applications to
the United States.

On April 3, General Homma sent a request that the commanders surrender. When he got no response, he ordered the most violent
strike in the war thus far. The air and land assault on the Second
Corps thundered across Bataan for two days as the men retreated,
leaving behind the dead and injured, the moaning and cursing men
who were missing limbs or had been smeared into trees or were
staring into pulsing open holes at their own gut sacks. On April 8,
most of the soldiers retreated to Mariveles Bay, dismantled their
weapons, and waited for the island's new rulers to appear. Some
commanders gave their men the option of surrendering or scam-
pering off into the jungle. Several detachments, finding themselves
surrounded by the enemy, disappeared into the thickets, refugees in
a strange land.

Among these detachments were Edwin Ramsey and Joe Barker,
the latter so emaciated he now wore his West Point ring on his
thumb. The two had been cut off from their unit and found themselves surrounded, hiding in the thick jungle. But the concussions
had stopped. The woods had fallen silent. Perhaps Bataan had fallen.

"You thinking what I'm thinking?" Ramsey asked.

"I don't see how it could be anything else," Barker said. "We'll
find out soon enough."

"What'll you do?" Ramsey asked.

"Don't suppose I'd last long in a prison camp," Barker said. "Surrendering doesn't appeal to me."

On April 9, Gen. Edward King, a Georgia native whose grandfather fought for the Confederacy, was thinking of Robert E. Lee's surrender at Appomattox Court House as he rode to meet General Homma. Four months of warfare had killed some six thousand Americans and thirty thousand Filipinos. Of the remaining soldiers, only 25 percent were considered combat ready. One general had sent headquarters a handwritten note from the field saying only half his command was even capable of fighting and the rest were so sick or tired they could not launch even a mild attack. King felt he had no other choice. The commander of the US and Philippine troops on Luzon finally gave up. But the orders never reached Ramsey and Barker.

They divided the few supplies they had left and shook hands.

"No matter what happens, we stick together," Barker said.

"Agreed," said Ramsey.

The remaining seventy-five thousand soldiers who did not flee into the jungle bent their rifle barrels in the crooks of *dao* trees, disposed of any Japanese money or photographs that might make it appear they'd looted a dead imperial soldier, and sat in the shade, white flags hanging limp from gun stocks, waiting. When the enemy finally arrived, they tried to follow orders. One infantryman watched as a Japanese soldier with two stars over his pocket screamed something at a Filipino fighter and the man saluted. That must've been the wrong move, because the officer brought his knee up and slammed it into the testicles of the Filipino, who fell to the ground writhing. The soldier then emptied his pistol into the prostrate Filipino. The Americans, rooted by their fear, could only watch.

Those who could stand on their own two feet were herded like cows down a hill, then divided into groups of one hundred, stripped of their rings and watches and pens, and forced into two columns, Americans on the right side of the road, Filipinos on the

Along the Bataan Death March, on which these prisoners were photographed, their hands were tied behind their backs. The march was from Bataan to the prison camp at Cabanatuan. *National Archives and Records Administration*

left. They still didn't understand the guttural shouts of their captors, but they'd learn soon enough.

"*Kurah!*" the Japanese soldiers shouted. "*Speedo!*"

Get moving, now. They had no idea where they were going, how long the march would be, what would happen once they arrived. They just marched, bearded and bedraggled prisoners as far as the eye could see down the rural Old National Road, stone and coral and ankle-deep sand, afraid they'd get their heads pounded if they didn't. They marched up the bayside highway, daydreaming of pot roast and rib-eye steak smothered with gravy, past their own bombed-out jeeps and smoldering tanks, through blinding dust and oppressive heat that soared above ninety degrees. The humidity was so thick it felt like walking through cellophane. They had no food or water, and many pairs of them carried their wounded comrades suspended in bedsheets hanging from bamboo poles, like pigs at a barbecue. Those who fell on the roadside from exhaustion were bayoneted and left where they fell. The Filipinos and Americans tried to bury their friends, but their new captors soon tired of waiting. The highway was littered with bodies. Word spread of a Japanese cleanup squad taking up the rear, bayoneting those too sick or tired to keep walking. Right foot, left foot, mile after mile, days into nights into days, four then five then six. They sucked sweat off their dirty fingers and filled their canteens in a slough occupied by a dead and bloated caribou. They marched through barrios where Filipinos wept at the sight, offered rice and coconut and whatever they had, and were driven back by the soldiers. They stopped to spend the night at a schoolyard ringed by barbed wire and slept on fly-covered human feces and bloody entrails left by the preceding groups the night before. They stopped sweating and then stopped producing saliva. The sun made blisters on their skin, and the cloud of dust hanging over the road caked their ears and beards. They stole the socks off dead patriots to protect their own feet from more blisters. Some with dysentery soiled themselves, then dealt with the dreaded chafing. Some grew deranged from dehydration and made the mistake of asking their captors for water, receiving instead a rifle butt to the mouth or ribs. Japanese soldiers in trucks would sometimes drive by the columns, randomly lancing soldiers with their twenty-inch bayonets, which were more like swords, or whipping them with lengths of rope. Men died with prayers on their lips.

Sixty-five miles they walked on the highway to nowhere.

16

SPIES

Independent guerrilla organizations sprang up across Manila, and the soldiers and ROTC boys who had escaped Bataan were forming their own groups, building mountain hideouts and learning whom among the local Filipino population they could trust. Japanese soldiers were crawling across the open city, so returning to Manila was unimaginable. What they needed was a way to communicate.

The commander of one of the organizations asked Joey if she'd like to work as a courier. She'd simply walk from place to place carrying secret communication between units organizing in north Luzon and the resistance in Manila. They also wanted Joey to bring back word on resistance activity in the countryside, which could then be relayed to American submarines off the coast.

Joey accepted the assignment and began striking out into the city, then to the perilous mountains, praying no one caught on. The problem was the Japanese sentries stationed throughout the city. They were suspicious of everything. And the military police had begun beating citizens suspected of spying. An outfit of military police known as the Kempeitai performed savage interrogations at Fort Santiago in the walled city. American soldiers who had escaped the death march had a price on their heads: five pesos each, dead or alive. Some of them escaped only to be captured later. They would testify to the torture. One, Cpl. Walter Chatham Jr. of the air corps, was caught after escaping Bataan and interrogated. He didn't know anything of importance about US plans, but the Kempeitai beat him with a blackjack and baseball bat, then clamped his hands to a table, drove bamboo slivers under his fingernails, and set fire to them. When he passed out from the pain, they splashed water on him and started again.

The guerrillas operating in the mountains were a ragtag but exceptional bunch. Among them was Capt. Russell Volckmann, a West Point graduate from Iowa, who refused to surrender after Bataan fell.

When things were looking dim, he appealed to Gen. William Brougher. "Sir, I'm still in pretty good physical shape—I have a lot of fight left in me," Volckmann recalled saying.

"Sure thing," Brougher said. "I'll report you missing in action on a patrol. If you try, the best of luck to you."

Volckmann and his friend Capt. Donald Blackburn, from Florida, made an escape to North Luzon with the help of friendly Filipinos. They joined up with other American and Filipino officers in the mountains, who informed them of the developing guerrilla structure. Capt. Ralph Praeger was active in Cagayan Province and Apayao. A Philippine governor named Roque Ablan had refused to surrender and now commanded a large guerrilla unit in the northwest. Robert Lapham, a reserve lieutenant in the army, was organizing some thirteen thousand fighters in Luzon's central plains and pulling off ambitious sabotage operations. Volckmann saw the need for more organization among the various units, so he decided to divide North Luzon into seven geographical districts and put in place a typical military structure of command in each district. This provided a tight communication system.

One of the biggest challenges to the units were spies and informers. Brilliantly, the Japanese hired local mayors or other government officials, then plied them with money to hire their own network of spies, who were offered payouts if they turned in important information on guerrilla activities. If that didn't work, or if the Japanese learned of local townsfolk or villagers cooperating with the Americans, they would hold public beheadings to send a message of fear through the populace.

The Japanese in large part had cut off news from the rest of the world, starting by rewiring all shortwave radios, which locals referred to as castration. If you owned a shortwave radio, you had to purchase a license from the government and pay an annual fee. Of course no one destroyed those records, so the Japanese knew every family who owned one. They broadcast a demand that all radios be brought in, and hired Filipino technicians to remove the shortwave coils so the radio could only receive AM signals. The newspapers had all but stopped publication, and those that kept printing, besides underground newspapers like the *Free Philippines*, were monitored by the Japanese and used as a vehicle for pro-Japanese propaganda. So one of the few ways citizens got unembellished reports on the war was from the guerrillas, some of whom had secret radios and even communicated with MacArthur in Australia. The guerrillas relied on Joey and other couriers to dispatch the news to the people.

At first, Joey carried the messages inside her hair, which she twisted and curled and bunched up in a chignon. Her techniques of getting the messages from place to place were up to her; the guerrillas told her that if she was caught, they'd never heard of her. One day she happened to be struck by the feeling that she needed to change her hiding place. The same day a Japanese sentry tugged on her hair, and her ponytail came loose.

She often tucked messages between two pairs of socks, and if she was stopped and asked to remove her socks for a search, she simply peeled both pairs off at once. Other times she carried the messages in hollowed-out fruit in a basket and pretended to be a street vendor.

She walked miles for the underground, hiding her face behind a veil and her secrets behind her stigma, the whole time wondering how long the war would last and what would happen once she was again an outcast.

17

PROMISE

The general wrote the words on the back of an envelope as he rode in a private train car toward the seaside Australian city of Adelaide. Reporters now knew MacArthur had escaped Corregidor, and they'd be waiting. Roosevelt had broken the news at a press conference three days before, knowing full well that the Axis would interpret the move as the abandonment of the Philippines. For three months and ten days, the general had held the Japanese at bay on Luzon, and his retreat would appear more surrender than regrouping. "I know that every man and woman in the United States admires with me General MacArthur's determination to fight to the finish with his men in the Philippines," the president said. "But I also know that every man and woman is in agreement that all important decisions must be made with a view toward the successful termination of the war. Knowing this, I am sure that every American, if faced individually with the question as to where General MacArthur could best serve his country, could come to only one answer."

MacArthur, he said, was now in command of everything, including sea and air forces, east of Singapore in the southwestern Pacific. The reaction was immediate and optimistic: Americans felt the dashing MacArthur was up to the task of stopping Japan's push southward and the late move to high command was some indication that intelligence officers now saw evidence that the tides of war in the Pacific were beginning to turn. The New York Stock Exchange even registered a spike when the news broke.

The general needed the right message, not only for Americans back home. He needed to send a message to his men—Filipinos and Americans alike—still fighting on Bataan and Corregidor and to the beloved inhabitants of the Philippine Islands, his second home. He needed to encourage them to keep fighting, to never give in to the occupiers.

"The President of the United States ordered me to break through the Japanese lines and proceed from Corregidor to Australia for the purpose, as I understand it, of organizing the American offensive against Japan, a primary object of which is the relief of the Philippines," he wrote. "I have come through and I shall return."

I shall return. These became the most famous words spoken during the war in the Pacific, and they lit a fire in Filipino hearts, becoming a battle cry against an impossible foe. Soon after MacArthur delivered the words, American subs began supplying Philippine guerrillas with branded materials. Gum, chocolate bars, matchboxes, buttons, playing cards, all printed with MacArthur's solemn promise.

18

BELEAGUERED

All night on April 8 and all day on April 9, the refugees from Bataan poured into Corregidor by boat, *banca*, raft, or on anything that could float. General Wainright had ordered that no troops be brought to Corregidor except one infantry unit and the army nurses, but these sad and tired stragglers refused to capitulate. Major General Moore assigned the new troops to tactical employment. The night sky on April 9 glowed red for hours as the Japanese blew up ammunition stores and bomb-laden vessels in the harbor.

With their new turf on Bataan under control, the Japanese rushed guns into place on the beaches, trained them on Corregidor, and began pounding away. The Corregidor guns were set to return fire on the beaches, but General Wainwright ordered them to hold fire. American prisoners of war now snaked along the roads of Bataan, and two nearby base hospitals were filled with sick and wounded US soldiers.

It seemed only a matter of time before the Japanese attempted a landing at Corregidor, but Moore was determined to hold the Rock for as long as possible. Soon, on April 11, five Japanese landing barges appeared off one of the points on Bataan's shoreline, hugging the shore and headed for the bay. Three Corregidor batteries opened fire and drove the boats back out of sight.

On April 12, General Wainwright issued these words to his troops on the Rock:

> Corregidor can and will be held. There can be no question of surrendering this mighty fortress to the enemy. It will be defended with all the resources at our command. Major General George F. Moore, commanding general of Fort Mills, is wholeheartedly with me in the unalterable decision to hold this island together with its auxiliary forts.
>
> I call upon every person in this fortress—officer, enlisted man, or civilian—to consider himself from this time onward as a member of a team which is resolved to meet the enemy's challenge each hour of every night and day.
>
> All men who have served here before will remain at their posts, while those who have come from Bataan will be assigned to appropriate tasks and battle stations. It is essential above all that the men who have joined us from the mainland promptly rid themselves of any defeatist attitude which they may have and consider themselves a part of this fighting unit.
>
> Bataan has fallen—but Corregidor will carry on! On this mighty fortress—a pearl of a great price on which the enemy has set his covetous eyes—the spirit of Bataan will continue to live!

The bombs fell daily, pulverizing the little island. One evening around 10:00 PM, a large group of men had congregated outside Malinta Tunnel, against orders, and a heavy shell fell in their midst. The bang launched the group into the air, killing them instantly. There were about fifty casualties.

On April 20, reports from guerrillas reached Moore that the enemy was assembling a large landing force on the east coast of Bataan. Time was short.

April 29 was Emperor Hirohito's birthday.

"As anticipated," Moore wrote, "the enemy decided to celebrate."

The bombs started falling at 7:30 AM. The 260th air-raid alarm sounded on the island, signaling the start of a nightmare that wouldn't end.

0800: Extremely heavy shelling at both portals of
 Malinta Tunnel and North dock.
0821: Enemy shelling Topside while observation plane
 overhead adjusts fire.
0923: Bombs dropped on west end of Corregidor.
0935: Battery Ramsey and H-60th bombed. Fire started
 below Middleside Incinerator.
0957: Middleside barracks bombed; some men injured.
0958: Enemy shelling near North Point.
1002: Two ammunition dumps at Topside exploding.

All day long. The next day, too. And the next. During one five-hour period, twelve 240-millimeter shells per minute—or thirty-six hundred total—rained down on Topside. The dust was so bad it blinded the spotters.

The beach defense installations on the north side of the island were ruined. The trees and natural vegetation had been blown to hell, and the ground was covered with powdered dust. Barbed wire and land mines had been blasted away. Communication lines were down. The Japanese had somewhere in the neighborhood of 422 guns in Bataan firing on Corregidor, and in the last ten days, they had launched more than 200,000 shells at the island.

At 10:30 PM on May 5, the radio crackled to the beach defense commander: "Prepare for probable landing attack." Two hours later, a Marine Corps runner sprinted into the H Station, breathless. He'd come from North Point. Enemy landing. "Probably six hundred men," he said.

A group of soldiers formed a line in the darkness across Kindley Field Water Tank Hill. They weren't done fighting. As the Japanese moved forward, a two-gun battery on the tail of the island opened fire, catching them by surprise and killing many with 193 rounds. Spotlights swung onto the landing crafts, and gunners were able to assault the vessels and the men aboard. Ten thousand Japanese soldiers followed in the second wave, and the fighting was intense as they disembarked and struggled to climb ashore. Soldiers fired on them in the moonlight. More landings followed at Infantry Point, but a counterattack drove them back. Soon soldiers were retreating for Malinta Tunnel.

General Wainwright radioed a message to President Roosevelt. "Our flag on this beleaguered island fortress still flies," it said.

FDR wrote back: "In spite of all the handicaps of complete isolation, lack of food and ammunition, you have given the world a shining example of patriotic fortitude and self-sacrifice.

"The American people ask no finer example of tenacity, resourcefulness, and steadfast courage. The calm determination of your leadership in a desperate situation sets a standard of duty for our soldiers throughout the world. . . . You and your devoted followers have become the living symbols of our war aims and the guarantee of victory."

Wainwright paced back and forth in Malinta Tunnel all night. By daylight, the Japanese soldiers were five hundred yards from the tunnel's east entrance. He had to make up his mind, which was still reeling with the task of trying to find ways and means of dodging what seemed inevitable. He walked into his own headquarters and called General Moore and Brig. Gen. Lewis Beebe inside. He had come to a decision.

"We can't hold out very much longer," Wainwright told them. "Maybe we could last through this day, but the end certainly must come tonight. It would be better to clear up the situation now, in daylight."

At the threshold of capture, Wainwright composed his last message to MacArthur:

> I feel it is my duty to the nation and my troops to end this useless slaughter. There is apparently no relief in sight. American and Filipino troops have engaged and held the enemy for nearly five months.
>
> We have done our full duty for you and for our country. We are sad but unashamed. I have fought for you to the best of my ability from Lingayen Gulf to Bataan to Corregidor, always hoping relief was on the way.
>
> Goodbye, General, my regards to you and our comrades in Australia. May God strengthen your arm to insure ultimate success of the cause for which we have fought side by side.

The morning sun revealed a once lush island now pulverized to a treeless desert littered with bodies. The Japanese had lost more than four thousand soldiers, but they'd managed to land tanks on Corregidor. General Wainwright met with Major General Moore and said he was prepared to surrender, considering the heavy casualty toll from the night of fighting. He'd give up the fortified islands at noon. He ordered Moore to destroy the entire armament by then, along with all records, secret maps, papers, correspondence, and diaries.

Wainwright also told Moore to lower the flag on Corregidor, burn it, and replace it with a white flag.

At noon, the American flag, which had been shot down twice and replaced during the siege, was burned and replaced by a white flag of truce. Despite the flag, the Japanese continued firing and dive-bombing.

The two men and their aides drove under a white flag to meet Japanese commanders. They left the car at the base of the Kindley Field Water Tank Hill and began the slow walk up. All around them

Surrender of American troops at Corregidor, Philippine Islands, May 1942.
National Archives and Records Administration

were the dead and dying. It looked to Moore to be a ratio of three Japanese soldiers for every one American or Filipino.

Wainwright met General Homma and surrendered. The Japanese put the prisoners on a boat and shipped them across the blue bay to Manila and paraded them through the city, making a mockery of the men. Wainwright was forced to walk past his defeated, pathetic soldiers. Despite being malnourished, battered, and injured, they struggled to their feet and stood at attention for their general.

19

TAKEN

The priests wept when Bataan fell, but they thought Corregidor would hold. They watched from the roof of the Ateneo as wave after wave of Japanese bombers assaulted the island, twenty-five miles away. The bombs rattled windows. Not one square yard of the island was without scar. The fathers snapped photographs of the planes over the island, then more when the Japanese navy steamed into Manila Bay. They listened to *Voice of America* reports on a hidden shortwave radio, but the good news was sparse.

Father Fred Julien, the La Salette priest now marooned in a war-torn city, had been keeping a diary filled with pictures of Japanese war planes and descriptions of what he had seen and heard since the invasion began. Besides that, he had jotted down detailed accounts of two Americans who had escaped during what was now being called the Bataan Death March and had then sought shelter at the Ateneo. The fathers helped hide Pfc. Clayton Rollins and Lt. James Atwell inside the compound until they were able to smuggle them out in the darkness and help the boys get to the mountains of Antipolo. The diary was Father Julien's secret, and he kept it hidden in his trouser belt, under his cassock.

Father Julien had taken to caring for another priest who was ill and interned at the University of Santo Tomas. He'd slip on a scarlet armband, which allowed relatively free movement in the city, and walk to the marketplace to collect donated items for his friend, then pass them through the fence at Santo Tomas. But the armband was illegal; it had been stolen off a commandant's desk. Father Julien prayed no one interrogated him about the band, but he kept up his trips to visit his friend and weekly ventures to offer Mass at a chapel on a palatial estate outside of town.

The trips were risky. Soldiers patrolled every street in the city around the clock, and the stories of their brutality had reached the Ateneo. The fathers heard stories of soldiers splitting heads open like melons, of soldiers pulling teeth and cutting tongues out, of suspected spies being beheaded. A young soldier at the hospital had given Father Julien his diary, which described many atrocities.

The Japanese had already launched an intense investigation into Father John Hurley, the superior at the Ateneo, and they returned to campus every two or three days. A young man at the gate of the Ateneo would press a secret button beneath his desk, alerting the priests on the third floor that the Japanese had arrived. Hurley, who had hung a sign outside his door that said CONTAGIOUS DISEASE, would quickly climb into bed and pretend to be ill.

Father Julien was returning to the Ateneo one day after a respite at the chapel outside of town. As he walked through the gate with his illegal armband and secret diary, a woman whispered. He recognized her from before. It was Josefina Guerrero.

"Do you have anything you shouldn't have?" she asked. "The Japanese are here searching for contraband."

"My diary," he whispered.

"Give it to me," she said. "Quickly."

He reached into his robe for the diary, but a military policeman grabbed him and escorted him over to the barracks, where about forty priests lived. Military police were searching everything. He tried to hide the small book, but one of the soldiers found it and flipped through the pages until he came to the photographs of Japanese planes bombing and strafing.

"War, war, you write," the soldier said.

Julien tried to explain that it was for his mama and papa back home.

The man put the diary on a stack of confiscated material.

"Anyone touch, we kill," one of the soldiers said.

Father Julien was scared to death. If they found out what he had written, or if they found the soldier's account of the atrocities, he feared he'd be killed. When they weren't looking, he grabbed the diary and hustled to the toilet, where he ripped out all the pages containing pictures or descriptions of war. He tore them into tiny pieces and flushed them down the toilet, then returned the book to the stack. He was amazed that no one noticed.

The next morning, Japanese soldiers arrived at the Ateneo and ordered the priests to pack one bag each. They were driven across the city and unloaded at Santo Tomas Internment Camp, where they slept that night on the concrete gymnasium floor. They woke at 2:00 AM and were forced onto a train for the forty-mile journey to a prison camp at Los Baños. Some would never make it back.

20

PLEDGE

The black limousine pulled to the curb on Manhattan's busy Fifth Avenue, outside St. Patrick's Cathedral. The back door opened, and out stepped Manuel Quezon, who looked out of place against the New York grit in his bright white suit, scarlet pocket square, and white wingtips. It was just before Low Mass at 8:00 AM, and the Philippine president was trailed by his wife and two young daughters, Maria Aurora, nicknamed Baby, and Zeneida. The party was greeted by Monsignor Joseph F. Flannelly, administrator of the cathedral, and Bishop John F. O'Hara, military delegate to the Catholics in the armed forces.

They were shown inside the neo-Gothic cathedral and seated facing the throne.

Archbishop Francis J. Spellman, who had entered the sanctuary earlier, was kneeling at the prie-dieu at the altar. When the party was seated, he was vested and began Mass.

Monsignor Flannelly extended a greeting to President Quezon.

"It is a very special privilege that I have this morning of welcoming to this Mass in the name of the Most Reverend Archbishop of New York the Hon. Manuel Quezon, President of the Philippines, and his family," Flannelly said. "Mr. President, I use the word welcome, but perhaps there is no need for it, for this is God's house, and whether a child of God be a part of the North, South, East, or West, he is always welcome here. And then in addition you have a second

75

claim on this great cathedral of New York, because you are of the Household of the Faith. There is, therefore, added joy in bringing you into this House of God today, because of the fact that you are a member, that you are of the Household of the Faith. And when we think of your people today, the people whom you represent, when we think of them today, stricken as they are, we see the great ray of hope in this fact alone, that you, their leader, are a man of ideals, you their leader are a man of Christian ideals. Today we offer up this Mass for you and with you for your people. We pray for mercy and we pray that mercy may be speedy. And we do thank God today that you and your people have that faith, have those ideals which will draw down from heaven the mercy that we all need."

Bishop O'Hara, former president of the University of Notre Dame, offered the sermon, then addressed Quezon from the pulpit in closing.

"A few years ago, in a prophetic utterance, Dr. Carlos Romulo stated that the security of a small nation lies in its remaining unnoticed or uncoveted," the bishop said. "In a world in which for the moment injustice abounds, Dr. Romulo's beautiful nation could not remain unnoticed. Our own nation had been enriched and inspired by the loyalty and brilliant courage of the citizens of that nation who stood shoulder to shoulder with us on Bataan and Corregidor. And to you, Mr. President, with every American, we endorse and repeat our own President's pledge, that we will return and will be proud to help you restore liberty to the only Christian nation in the Orient.

"Our task must be fulfilled without hatred. Justice and charity alone can bring peace; justice alone can give us the proper fruits of victory. Hatred can never produce anything but destruction. Only justice that abounds more than that of the Pharisees can bring the peace of God."

When the service was over, Archbishop Spellman, a man who would hold true to that promise, approached the party and stopped to speak with them. They each kissed his ring, then left through the front doors, and the archbishop then turned and knelt again at the prie-dieu and resumed his prayers.

21

I'M A LEPER

The bombs make the headlines, but war is made up of a million tiny moments that slip by unnoticed but for those in the thick. Joey received another assignment, her most dangerous yet. She was asked to map the Japanese fortifications and gun emplacements on the Manila waterfront.

The port area and much of the land around Manila Bay was heavily guarded and to do her work, she knew she'd have to infiltrate the fortified zones again and again. The past year had been the hardest of her life. There was a chronic food shortage to begin with, and medicine was nearly impossible to get. Prices on the black market had soared. Without medicine, her disease overtook her. Red blotches appeared on her face, arms, and back.

But she was beginning to notice an advantage to the swollen nodes and skin discoloration. The Japanese soldiers, who had been so aggressive when she didn't appear to be afflicted, now wanted nothing to do with her. All it took was seeing the blotches, and the sentries practically fled. The Japanese were culturally horrified of a disease they misunderstood. They thought leprosy was highly communicable and feared being anywhere near someone afflicted. In a way, it became Joey's passport. She began to embrace the disease and use it as a tool, better than any weapon.

"Unclean," she'd say if a sentry approached.

It was not uncommon for sentries to force suspected spies or couriers to undress and submit to a full-body search, but Joey never had to relent.

"I'm a leper," she'd say.

"Go, now!" the frightened soldier would say.

She made her way along Dewey Boulevard and around the banks of the silver Manila Bay, in clear view of the barren hulk of Corregidor, making note of where gun emplacements were before heading home to jot them down on her hand-drawn map. The information was crucial, she knew, but she had no idea how timely it would be, how soon the bombs would start falling.

A puppet government had grown in Manuel Quezon's absence. In early 1942, before Bataan and Corregidor fell, General Homma appointed a stand-in government to run the country. These collaborators soon declared war on the United States and Great Britain, and a few thousand Filipinos signed up to join the Makapili, a militant group established to aid the Japanese when the Americans returned.

While MacArthur felt betrayed by the puppet government and swore to "run to earth every disloyal Filipino who has debased his country's cause," the country regained a sense of stability. Much of society was not affected by Japanese rule, outside of occasional hassles and severe food shortages. The city rocked along on a steady beat, fishermen navigating the shores in *bancas*, peasants carrying bags of rice down dirt roads, the faithful celebrating Mass inside crumbling churches. Flames of independence flickered in all their hearts, but the timing had to be right.

In the shadows of the steeples and in the cobblestone alleyways and in the mountains outside the city, though, the guerrillas were plotting, coding, looking for their chance to strike. The boys from the Ateneo, some of them now banded into an outfit called Hunters ROTC, were pulling daring pranks on the Japanese—the best they could do. They'd sneak up to enemy trucks on the corner of Avenida Rizal and Azcarraga and pour sugar into their fuel tanks. The trucks would run fifty yards and stall out. When sugar got too expensive, they used sand. When they recognized the need for guns, the Hunters raided the University of the Philippines armory in Manila. The trick was avoiding the sentries, which sometimes was just luck. After one raid, a Philippine Military Academy (PMA) cadet named Gustavo Ingles was on a *karetela*, or horse carriage, that was loaded with ammunition. Another cadet named Terry Adevoso was holding a bundle of bullets. The sentry stopped the cart and demanded to know what was in the package.

"Bullets," Adevoso said. "Bullets and guns."

The soldier thought it was hilarious. He told them to move along without checking the parcels.

For a raid on the armory at Union College, the Hunters commandeered a truck, loaded it with guns, and took off for Antipolo, the unit's hideout east of Manila. As the truck passed the sentry post, the boys got out and bowed deeply to the guards, who seemed uninterested in checking the contents and waved them along. But the truck wouldn't start again. Their friends, a diversionary group on hand if something went awry, watched nervously from across the street. But the guards found the Hunters to be so courteous and respectful that they helped push the truck down the street until it started.

The boys developed a hatred for their occupiers. The war had disrupted life, but they were also disgusted by a foreign power now ruling a democratic city. They were stopped and frisked in the dark. They heard stories about their female friends being raped or assaulted. Their families were afraid. So they looked for ways, large and small, to strike back.

When Marcos Villa Agustin, who was a cabdriver and boxer before the war and now led a resistance unit called Marking's Guerrillas, heard that the Japanese were using American prisoners of war to build a bridge near Lumban, Laguna, and that the prisoners were so weak from hunger they were falling off the bridge, he organized a raid. Scouts borrowed a guitar and pretended to be strolling serenaders so they could get an idea of where the enemy was. Marking and forty of his best men raided Lumban Concentration Camp, shooting and hacking to death ten sentries. But only 1 of the 150 prisoners of war, Cpl. George Lightman of the Third Pursuit Squadron, dared to escape with the guerrillas.

The retaliation for the raids and sabotage came swiftly. The Japanese kidnapped two Hunters guards and tortured them until they revealed the unit's hiding place in Antipolo. They also formed a firing squad and shot to death ten American prisoners of war in front of the town's mayor and police chief as a scare tactic. The following morning, soldiers raided the Antipolo camp, killing one of the leaders, Mike Ver, a twenty-three-year-old engineering student from the Mapua Institute of Technology. The boys found him with a gaping hole in the side of his neck. The fight was suddenly real. Many of the young guerrillas gave up that day. The group that had grown to 250 fighters dropped to 30. Those who stayed started looking for vengeance.

They weren't good fighters at first. They had heart and a surplus of guts, but they lacked any real training. So they read books about guerrilla warfare—Mao Zedong and Lawrence of Arabia—and practiced guerrilla techniques in the jungle and figured out their own tactics. They wanted to fight, not wait on the Americans.

Those who remained part of the Hunters went to Pililia, a small town on the eastern bank of Laguna de Bay, east of Manila, where they learned that a Japanese convoy moving from Rizal to Laguna was expected to pass through soon. Sixteen young men and two Igorots, or mountain people, staked out their hiding places along a road that zigzagged through private property, near Kilometer 70. When the convoy came into view, the boys noticed that there were escorts on foot surrounding the trucks, walking as though they were on alert. The gunfire didn't last long. It was the first time Gustavo Ingles, the PMA cadet, ever heard the Japanese crying in pain, and over their dead, and it fueled his soul. They'd meant to take revenge for their friend, and they'd done so with gusto, without a single casualty.

Word began to spread about the Hunters and Marking's Guerrillas, and more boys signed on. Recruits came from Cavite, Batangas, Rizal, Laguna, and all the way from Candelaria, Quezon, seventy miles south. Over the course of the war, some five thousand men and women would join the Markings in combat. Even more served as home guards, providing intelligence and supplies when the guerrilla bands passed through town. Peasant farmers secretly brought rice and sugar to the camps. Church groups in Manila began to organize resistance inside chapels, under the guise of Christian worship, because the Japanese prohibited groups gathering in homes. They held rummage sales and collected old clothes secretly destined for the guerrillas. Couriers would arrive at midnight, retrieve the donations, and start the long journey to the mountain hideouts.

One band of young people at Cosmopolitan Church on General Luna Street joined the choir and began holding rehearsals three times a week, at 6:00 PM. Some engineering students from the University of the Philippines had reworked a radio, fixing it so it received *Voice of America* broadcasts transmitted from California and Hawaii. Choir rehearsal was a front, a chance to simply gather to listen to the broadcasts, which volunteers then typed on onionskins and passed around to friends. Their mission was to encourage their fellow citizens who might be leaning toward acquiescence.

To stunt the growth of the resistance, the Japanese redoubled efforts to convince Filipinos to give up. They tried propaganda, suggesting most of the islanders were cooperating with the Japanese to build that shining hope for the future, the Great East Asia Co-prosperity Sphere, but often sent mixed messages that had the opposite effect than intended. One broadcast from Tokyo, for instance, proclaimed, "In central Luzon, 1,300 bandits surrendered in February and were now cooperating wholeheartedly with Japan. American and Filipino bandits, who were active in Northern Luzon are almost wiped out, and the rest—about a hundred—have fled to the mountains, where they will starve to death. . . . It has become clear that the day is not far away when the whole Philippines will cooperate wholeheartedly with Japan." But the guerrillas knew better, and so did many ordinary Filipinos.

When propaganda didn't work, the Japanese tried bribery and treachery. When that didn't work, they began making wholesale arrests, torturing suspects at Fort Santiago and making those who wouldn't break dig their own graves. Thousands of soldiers surrounded Mount Canumay in Tanay, Rizal, for two months, trying to flush Marking out of hiding. But they didn't know the terrain like the guerrillas and eventually realized the native commando had escaped.

Soldiers came for Esperanza Enriquez one morning and took her to a house in the rural northeastern section of Luzon. Her husband was a guerrilla leader, and soldiers had been combing the hillsides, hunting him. Each night the soldiers would bring in a man badly beaten and ask if it was her husband. They forced her to write copies of the same letter, over and over.

> Dear Manolo,
> Please come home now. The children are missing you very much. The Japanese army are very kind. Peter was very sick and they gave us medicine and plenty of gifts for the children, including school supplies. They promised me they will not harm you. Lay down your arms and come home soon. Everything is fine and normal. Come home and experience the life we are enjoying now. Love, Mommy.

The soldiers dropped the letters all over the mountains, trying to entice Manolo to surrender. A few days later, a servant at the house, who had been fetching water, slipped Esperanza a note. It was from her husband.

> Mommy, don't be frightened. I am only four houses away from you. We are taking care of you. If they hurt you, we will come and kill them all.

All the antiresistance effort only deepened the resentment and strengthened the guerrillas' commitment to driving the occupiers mad. Soon they had infiltrated the police department, and the friendly officers would tip off the resistance if the Japanese police were planning a raid.

By August 1944, eighteen million Filipinos lived in the islands, and they were being watched by about four hundred thousand Japanese soldiers. But 180,000 Filipinos—1 in 100—were in some way serving the resistance. The resistance ranks were growing daily, and they would number nearly 250,000 by the spring of 1945.

They were middle-class citizens and even society women whose allegiances were with the Americans. They owned cinemas and worked for the YMCA and made fun of their new masters by mocking them in Tagalog. They talked about underground activities at pretend dinner meetings and funneled food to the warriors in the mountains and messages to General MacArthur. In fact, radio traffic picked up to an unusual clip, with nearly four thousand messages being logged each month at the Australian headquarters for the US Army Forces in the Far East. They sent transcripts of secret executive sessions of the puppet regime, guest lists of visitors to the Manila Hotel, movements of Japanese armed forces. Hundreds of groups sprang to life in the islands, with names like the Civilian Liberation Volunteers and Farmer Labor Auxiliary Service and the Heroes of Democracy. Their loyalty rode with MacArthur and Quezon, and when Quezon died from tuberculosis at a cure cottage in Upstate New York on August 1, 1944, it rode with MacArthur alone.

The general's submarines supplied them with morale in the form of transmitters and equipment and matchbooks that reinforced his promise to return. More and more, they could monitor US troop movements, feel the pulse of the war, and the word spread like prairie fire when, on June 6, 1944, allied troops landed along a fifty-mile stretch of French coastline to fight the Nazis. The bold statistics of the effort, a mighty show of force, were repeated in astonished tones on Calle Real and around Plaza Goiti and on the quiet corners of Escolta Street: more than 5,000 ships and 13,000 aircraft ran support for 160,000 allied troops.

"The eyes of the world are upon you," they heard Gen. Dwight D. Eisenhower, supreme commander of the Allied forces, say. "The hopes and prayers of liberty-loving people everywhere are with you."

22

VENGEANCE

Father Fred Julien and the Catholic priests being held at the Los Baños Internment Camp, snug between Mount Makiling and Laguna de Bay, never heard about D-day. Their secret radio was still at the Ateneo, for all they knew. The days of 1944 bled together, and a dismal routine set in among the 126 priests, several nuns, and other missionaries and their families in a barracks they called Little Vatican. They were kept separate from the two thousand or so Americans, British, Australians, Dutch, Norwegians, Poles, Italians, and Canadians, most of them civilians rounded up after the outset of war. They divided themselves into committees and were each assigned simple tasks like mending, carpentry, and policing.

But with each passing month, food rations were diminished. The twice-daily meals were mostly an ice-cream-scoop-sized portion of rice gruel with a little hog grease on top. One man and his wife had volunteered to be part of an experiment—getting weighed every two weeks at the camp hospital—with the hopes that the Japanese doctors might be humanitarian enough to be saddened by their weight loss and order an increase in rations. After a few months of weighing in, the man and his wife realized they were losing twelve to fourteen pounds every two weeks. They stopped volunteering when she dropped below eighty pounds and he dropped below one hundred.

The prisoners were burying two or three of their own per day, deaths caused by starvation or related diseases. Some of the priests took to eating banana peels directly out of the hog slop. They ate dogs, cats, snakes—anything they could catch—and they made up songs like schoolchildren to fight the tedium, hoping against hope that the Americans were on their way.

> *Oh, we'll all have apple pie when they come*
> *Oh, we'll all have apple pie when they come*
> *Oh, I don't want to die*
> *Till we have that apple pie*
> *Till we have that apple pie when they come*

They were exhilarated when the airplanes began appearing in the sky, and they'd squint against the morning sunshine to try to make out the insignia on the tails. They watched, once, as an American plane was blasted out of the sky, and saw clearly the pilot's parachute mushroom as he descended into a thicket of trees. Japanese officers left the camp at Los Baños and rode horses into the jungle but failed to find the pilot. A few nights later, local guerrillas—Hunters, most likely—crawled under the barbed wire ringing the camp's perimeter and told the priests that they had rescued the pilot and needed civilian clothes to help him get back to friendly quarters. It worked.

Forty miles away in Manila, the guerrillas were being called to the hills. Word had reached the islands that the time to fight was drawing near, possibly before June. Filipinos brought their guns out from hiding and sharpened their bolos. Buried caches of artillery were unearthed on Bataan and shipped to fighters in central Luzon. The boy who tended to the pigs at the Ateneo came to Father Forbes Monaghan to resign his job.

"My country needs me," he told the priest.

Later, Monaghan was riding in a crowded streetcar when a sudden jerk hurled every standing passenger to the rear. One of them inadvertently tugged the coat of the man in front of him, revealing a shoulder belt packed with bullets. A police officer saw this and tapped the armed guerrilla.

"Get off with me at the next stop!" the Filipino officer said.

The guerrilla tapped him back.

"No," he said. "You get off at the next stop. There are six of us in this car."

The police officer got off at the next stop.

At Santo Tomas, where Joey continued to try to minister to the starving internees at great personal risk, a new visitor had arrived: Father John Hurley, the powerfully built, indomitable superior of the Jesuit mission. He had been evicted from the Ateneo and was even arrested and detained at Fort Santiago, but he had successfully defended himself and refused to collaborate with the Japanese. When he was finally ordered to Santo Tomas, the internees gave him a standing ovation.

Though they had been through much hardship, the internees at Santo Tomas were a feisty and ingenious bunch. More than the other war camps, perhaps, Santo Tomas had become a well-organized community with public health facilities, gardens, sports programs, access to goods and money on the outside, schooling, shops, shacks, and even somewhat regular entertainment. They knew how to make the best of a bad situation, as illustrated by tongue-in-cheek songs written and performed by internees, such as "Cheer Up, Everything's Going to Be Lousy":

I've plenty to be thankful for although it's hard to bear.
Things could be a darned sight worse, although I don't know where.
Don't think that I'm complaining, 'cause it's really not the case,
And, if I look disgusted, why, it's just my natural face.
I haven't a pot to cook in, but, at least I have a bed.
It may belong to the Red Cross, but, it's a place to lay my head.
So smile and show your dimples, they're worth their weight in gold.
You may as well my friends, before you know it you'll be old.

The most traumatic event had come in the first two months, when three men—an Australian engineer and two British merchant seamen—were executed for trying to escape.

But in the first two years, for the most part, the Japanese generally kept away from most internees. Internees took advantage of the lax oversight. Earl Hornbostel, whose father, Hans, survived the Bataan Death March and was a POW in another camp, was running a shortwave radio hidden in the projection room. But it wasn't until the guards found transcripts of news broadcasts from America that Hornbostel became a suspect and was sent to Fort Santiago for questioning. In reality, the transcripts were made outside of camp by a man living in San Juan, who would send transcripts to his father, also interned at Santo Tomas, on sheets of onionskin rolled up inside fountain pens. When questioned, the father fingered Hornbostel, probably to avoid torture.

When Hornbostel was transferred to Fort Santiago, where they made him stand facing a wall for hours before interrogation, the halls of the ancient Spanish compound still rang with the stories of defiant guerrillas.

Ramon Cabrera was a small, tough kid who played halfback on the football team at the Ateneo. At the start of the war, Cabrera had gotten to Bataan with the rest of the boys, fought hard, and survived the death march. He was imprisoned at Capas and, when released, joined the underground. He was soon caught and brought to Fort Santiago, and the Japanese secret police wanted him to cough up the names of the guerrillas with whom he was working. "I don't know any names," Cabrera said. So they beat him. They smashed his teeth out with a gun butt and broke his jaw. They burned his back with flatirons and tore off his fingernails. Still he refused to rat on his friends in the underground. When the Kempeitai brought Cabrera to the North Cemetery, they ordered him to dig his own grave. "Dig it yourself," he fired back. An officer drove a bayonet into him, and he fell to his knees. But when he looked up, he was smiling, blood bubbling from his mouth. He never did talk.

Carlos Malonzo, too, had been held at Fort Santiago. He was just eighteen when the Japanese invaded, and utterly indifferent about the new occupiers. But on his way to work one morning, he witnessed a Japanese sentry slap an old woman for failing to bow. Malonzo vowed a personal war. At first this involved staking out a Japanese supply facility, then patiently tunneling underground from an abandoned house across the street, then stealing thousands of pesos worth of supplies, which he sold on the black market. With the money he bought a radio transmitter and hired a Japanese-speaking interpreter and began broadcasting a regular program, *The Voice of Juan de la Cruz*, which could be heard all the way in San Francisco.

At the start of every program, Malonzo played the American and Philippine national anthems, followed by war news, and then offered a reward of fifty bottles of San Miguel for the capture or killing of the Japanese commander in the Philippines, the lowest of insults. The broadcast drove the occupiers mad, and they soon tracked Malonzo down in Pasay City. The Kempeitai at Fort Santiago tried to turn him. They offered him freedom if he would help spread Japanese propaganda. "Please thank the Japanese Military Administration for their offer to save my life," he told the interpreter. "But I cannot accept. In fact, if I have to do it all over again, I would do the same thing and even more." Not long after, he tried to escape and was caught. Soldiers bayoneted his feet, and he was bleeding when they returned him to his cell. "I'll do it again!" he shouted at the guards. When it came time for his execution, he told his cellmates at the fort to show no fear if their time came. "Never give them that satisfaction," he said, "but die with pride and dignity."

The fathers from the Ateneo were prisoners there, too, part of the crackdown on the Christian priests by the secret police. When Gustavo Ingles was sent for questioning, he counted ten priests from the Ateneo being held prisoner, all facing different charges, from possessing illegal photographs of Tokyo burning to stashing bayonets to spy activity. The remaining free fathers were close to being rounded up and shipped to Los Baños as well.

Hornbostel was court-martialed and sentenced to three years in Muntinlupa, which wasn't the worst prison. There were no Japanese; it was run by the Filipino staff that had been in place since before the war. In fact, it was run by Eriberto Misa Sr., the father of a guerrilla, and several Hunters were on staff.

23

LANDINGS

By March 1944, an aircraft rolled out of an American factory every 295 seconds. The American fleet of aircraft carriers had exploded from four in the Pacific in 1943 to almost one hundred a year later. American submarines had suffocated Japanese supply routes. In the ten months before October 1944, the Japanese had not sunk a single important US ship, and so depleted was Japan's air fleet that the Americans hopscotched island nations, completely bypassing Japanese air fields as troops jumped from island to island.

Since the decisive US victory at the Battle of Midway in June 1942, a month after Corregidor fell, MacArthur had stitched together an impressive string of triumphs. The Americans took Guadalcanal, then the Aleutian Islands, then Saipan, then Guam. In two months, he had pushed twelve hundred miles up Papua New Guinea and claimed Hollandia, where he was now moving his headquarters during Operation Reckless. In Tokyo, at Imperial Headquarters, planners used little red flags to illustrate the American movement on a wall map. Red flags spread to Finschhafen, westward along the New Guinea coast, to Saidor, Madang, Sansapor, and eastward to the Gilbert Islands, the Marshalls. The Americans had moved within one thousand miles of Mindanao, on the southern tip of the Philippine archipelago.

It was against this backdrop that MacArthur was summoned to Oahu on June 26, 1944, just before his sixty-fourth birthday, to meet with President Roosevelt and Adm. Chester Nimitz, commander in chief of the Pacific Fleet. MacArthur, late as usual, arrived at the USS *Baltimore* in a leather air force jacket and khaki slacks, saluted the quarterdeck, and went below to FDR's guest cabin. He didn't want to be here and had bellyached on the flight in about having to leave his post during war.

"Douglas, where do we go from here?" Roosevelt asked the general, who was now the Allied supreme commander of the South-West Pacific Area.

"Leyte, Mr. President, and then Luzon!" he replied. MacArthur had been singing the same tune since he abandoned Corregidor on the patrol torpedo boat in 1942, insisting that reclaiming the Philippines was strategically responsible to prepare for an attack on the Japanese mainland and, perhaps more important, was the honorable thing to do. But he was the only cheerleader for this plan. While not as passionate, Nimitz, perhaps the greatest naval commander in history, explained that Japan needed oil to continue operating, and its homeland was dry. So cutting off supply from the South Pacific, the Indies, and Indochina would strangle the emperor's effort.

"Cork that bottle, Mr. President," Nimitz said, "and Japan cannot go on fighting the war."

"How do we cork that bottle?" the president asked.

"Bypass the Philippines," Nimitz said. "Land on Formosa or even Okinawa. Interdict all Jap shipping with sea and air power. Collapse and surrender has to follow."

MacArthur was having none of it. His own honor was riding on liberating the people of the Philippines, even if it delayed troop movement toward Japan. He'd made a promise.

Roosevelt expressed concern about the human cost of taking the islands.

"National honor is a strong sentiment," he said. "Can you take the Philippines with the forces you have? I cannot spare anything for you . . . not when we've got Hitler on the run in Europe."

MacArthur, who knew when so much as a sparrow fell in the Philippines because of his communications with guerrillas, tried to put the president at ease.

"Mr. President, my losses would not be heavy, any more than they have been in the past," he said. "The days of the frontal attack are over. Modern infantry weapons are too deadly, and direct assault is no longer feasible. Only mediocre commanders still use it. Your good commanders do not turn in heavy losses."

As he climbed back onto his plane, bound for Australia, MacArthur declared to his staff, "We've sold it!"

Meanwhile, Manila was changing as the Japanese, who suspected the dual advance by MacArthur and Nimitz to the Philippines, ramped up for what Tokyo called "the decisive battle." Transport planes landed at Nielson and Nichols Fields on Luzon with Japanese commanders relocating their headquarters. Reinforcements were arriving on troopships in Manila Bay as part of the last-ditch imperial plan called Operation Victory. The military also gained a new and feared leader in Tomoyuki Yamashita, known as the Tiger of Malaya for his spectacular victories in Malaya and Singapore, which Winston Churchill called the "largest capitulation" in British military history.

Then, on the morning of September 21, the incredible happened. A boy, age twelve, was studying mathematics on the roof of Santo Tomas, where he and his family had been captive for nearly three years. He only heard the sound at first, a dull, indefinite humming in the air, a low vibration.

> The sound began to grow. And as it swelled into a road the windowpanes trembled till the concrete building started to shake. Out of the massy surge of clouds, the American bombers came, tier upon tier of them, flying high, flying low, an earth shaking armada of aeroplanes, glistening silver-white in the sun as they rode the air.
>
> One, two, three . . .

The prisoners began to count them.

Four, five, six . . .

Some internees ducked into the safety of the air-raid shelter but couldn't help sticking their heads out to watch the American bombers.

Seven, eight, nine . . .

The planes shifted formation like players on a football field. What grace. What timing.

Ten, eleven, twelve . . .

The people on the ground spotted Hellcats, Helldivers, and Avengers charging through the sky. American planes. When they came over land, bombs began to drop from their bellies and under-wing apparatus, bombs on which boys had written in chalk, ONLY THE BEGINNING, and they smashed the harbor defenses, the gun emplacements Joey Guerrero had so diligently mapped and turned over to the United States. The explosions shook the earth and sent plumes of dirt spraying skyward.

24

ADVANCE

The newspaper headline the next day was predictable: GREAT MANILA AIR BATTLE: US BOMBER FLEET WIPED OUT!

A joke developed in its wake:

What can shoot down more American aircraft than all the guns in the Japanese Combined Fleet? A new secret weapon?

No. The *Manila Herald*.

Unbeknownst to those in Manila, by late October, giant American guns aboard two US fleets were blazing, firing on Red Beach on the Island of Leyte, 550 miles southeast of the capital city. Soldiers fanned out, flushing snipers out of trees and routing them from foxholes. General MacArthur stood on the bridge of the *Nashville*, watching as the shoreline came into view, the same spot where in 1903 he had reported as a second lieutenant. He was as excited as a teenager going to his first dance, and he beamed in front of the cameras as he waded ashore. Roosevelt had already radioed him on the *Nashville*: "You have the nation's gratitude and the nation's prayers for success as you and your men fight your way back."

The general stood before a microphone and, over the crackle of volleys, gave an address to every Filipino within earshot of a short-wave radio:

> I have returned. By the grace of Almighty God our forces
> stand again on Philippine soil—soil consecrated in the

blood of our two peoples. We have come, dedicated and committed, to the task of destroying every vestige of enemy control over your daily lives, and of restoring, upon a foundation of indestructible strength, the liberties of your people.

At my side is your President, Sergio Osmena, worthy successor of that great patriot, Manuel Quezon, with members of his cabinet. The seat of your government is now therefore firmly re-established on Philippine soil.

The hour of your redemption is here. Your patriots have demonstrated an unswerving and resolute devotion to the principles of freedom that challenges the best that is written on the pages of human history. I now call upon your supreme effort that the enemy may know from the temper of an aroused and outraged people within that he has a force there to contend with no less violent than is the force committed from without.

Rally to me. Let the indomitable spirit of Bataan and Corregidor lead on. As the lines of battle roll forward to bring you within the zone of operations, rise and strike. Strike at every favorable opportunity. For your homes and hearths, strike! For future generations of your sons and daughters, strike! In the name of your sacred dead, strike! Let no heart be faint. Let every arm be steeled. The guidance of divine God points the way. Follow in His Name to the Holy Grail of righteous victory!

The move was in keeping with what Tokyo had predicted, and war planners were not displeased. They had set a trap, the Americans had steamed into it, and now it could be sprung. The Japanese Combined Fleet launched an attack that became known as the Battle of Leyte Gulf.

The plan was to decoy the US Third Fleet north, away from the San Bernardino Strait, while converging three forces on Leyte Gulf

Gen. Douglas MacArthur wades ashore during initial landings at Leyte,
Philippine Islands, in October 1944. *National Archives and Records Administration*

to attack the landing. But submarines of the US Seventh Fleet discovered the Japanese forces as they got into position southwest of
Leyte and sank two heavy cruisers on October 23. Two days later, at
the Surigao Strait, battleships and cruisers from the Seventh Fleet
destroyed C Force and forced the Second Attack Force to withdraw. The First Attack Force passed through the unguarded San
Bernardino Strait and inflicted heavy damage on the Seventh Fleet
escort carriers but withdrew unexpectedly just as they seemed ready
to attack the landing operations. In the north, off Cape Engaño, part
of the Third Fleet sank Japanese carriers while another part moved
south, attacking and pursuing the First Attack Force. The decisive
victory crippled the Japanese fleet. The invasion of the Philippines
was on.

Guerrillas joined the attack, and reports of slaughters soon
spread. Fighters on Leyte hacked drowning, dislodged Japanese sailors to pieces as they tried to crawl ashore. Eriberto Misa Jr. watched
as American planes bombed three Japanese navy ships in Balanacan

Bay in Marinduque. When the sailors swam to shore from the burning boats, guerrillas clubbed them to death. They then collected
maps and official-looking documents floating in the bay and carried
them to MacArthur on Leyte. Patrols at Yamashita's headquarters
turned up hidden machine guns and grenades on the property. Frus-
trated, Yamashita ordered the Kempeitai to comb the city and pun-
ish guerrillas. Men suspected of resistance activities were beheaded
in the streets.

But the activity didn't stop. Guerrillas attacked supply convoys
on the roads entering Manila, and food grew even scarcer. Prisoners
at Bilibid and Santo Tomas began to starve to death, but they sensed
the coming Americans. Father John Hurley, who had watched his

Two Coast Guard–manned LSTs open their great jaws in the surf that
washes on Leyte Island beach as soldiers strip down and build sandbag
piers out to the ramps to speed up unloading operations in 1944.
National Archives and Records Administration

body weight plummet from 208 pounds to 115, watched an American plane swoop in low and unleash thousands of leaflets, a few of which the internees got their hands on before the Japanese could pick them up. It read like a Christmas card and gave the prisoners a boost.

> The Commander-in-Chief, the Officers and the men of the American Forces of Liberation in the Pacific wish their gallant allies, the People of the Philippines, all the blessings of Christmas and the realization of their fervent hopes for the New Year. Christmas, 1944.

Meanwhile, the Kempeitai was ruthless and started rounding up European civilians and Filipinos who had friends and relatives in prison. They turned up at Malate Church and arrested three Irish priests, Father Forbes Monaghan among them. The secret police took the priests to an old Spanish house on Vito Cruz and tortured them until the priests were able to convince them they knew nothing. Of course, Monaghan knew lots. He knew about Lulu Reyes, who had assembled a truckload of rice, beans, sugar, peanuts, and salted fish for the priests and nuns at Los Baños and secreted in news about Ateneans in the underground who had died and about those who needed prayers. Lulu was friends with Joey Guerrero, too, who still took Mass daily where she could find it, but the petite spy had taken a hiatus from the resistance.

Joey's position had become so perilous that she was advised to disappear for a while. The guerrillas had learned that the Kempeitai had been asking around about her, and they suspected she was being shadowed. But when their interest had cooled, she went back to work.

Joey was lying in bed late one night in December when she heard an engine outside her house in Ermita. She peeked out the window and was startled to see a Japanese officer's car stopped out front with a white flag on the radiator cap. Her heart raced and she wondered why they had come. Maybe someone had ratted her out. Several female friends had already been rounded up and were detained at Fort Santiago.

Just then, there came a violent knocking at the door. She glanced around the house and quickly began hiding papers and other incriminating material. More knocking thundered through the house. She couldn't keep them waiting any longer, or they'd break the door down. She straightened herself and opened the door. The two officers stood erect in the darkness.

"May we come in?" one asked.

Sort of courteous for a Japanese officer, Joey thought. Without waiting, the men barged in. The second man looked too tall to be Japanese. When they entered the living room, the moonlight fell through the blinds onto the face of the tall man. He didn't *look* Japanese. Joey switched on the light and turned again to look at him. One man was clearly Filipino, and she recognized him as an officer in the underground. The other fellow was clearly Caucasian.

"You're an American!" she said.

When they closed the blinds, the guerrilla introduced Joey to the American. "This is the man you and I have been working under," he said. He gave her his alias; "Major Nicholson of the Eleventh Airborne," he said. She never knew who she had been working for, and she never learned his real name. The major congratulated her on her fine map of the gun emplacements on the waterfront. He had another request. The two men had brought along spare tires, which were actually crude incendiary devices. "Can we leave them here?" the American asked. Joey nodded, and the two took turns lugging the explosives in from the car and then disappeared again into the night.

The city was on edge, with new Japanese troops arriving every day. Hovering over the city was a grand sense that something big was about to happen. The guerrillas, meanwhile, were emboldened. While most sabotage had been confined to the provinces outside Manila in the past two years, daring resistance fighters had begun testing the Japanese inside the city limits. They fetched the spare tires from Joey Guerrero's house and set fire to a tanker in Manila Bay. Then they used more tires to torch Piers 5 and 7 at the port. After that, they set alight a steamer on the Pasig River that was loaded with rice and crude oil.

Joey feared the Kempeitai would track the sabotage to her house, to her. She felt like she was being followed, but she was never stopped for questioning. Near the end of January, she was summoned again by her superior. He had one more mission for her.

25

MAP

The map was crudely drawn but explicit enough. It clearly identified Blumentritt Railway Station and the Chinese Cemetery and the wide field in which the guerrillas had the day before discovered turned earth and freshly buried land mines, a last desperate attempt by the Japanese to end American lives. The previous maps the underground had supplied to the American soldiers advancing on the city from the north had indicated every mine and tank trap on the north side of the capital but did not include the new mines, which were buried between the Thirty-Seventh Infantry Division and Santo Tomas, where the internees were beginning to drop from starvation.

The soldiers of the Thirty-Seventh Division were weary, even if they'd enjoyed shore leave on Manus Island over the Christmas holiday. Their division commander, Gen. Robert S. Beightler, a citizen soldier and veteran of World War I, had predicted the Japanese would put up a desperate fight "since they have no place to which they can retreat." He was tired of issuing orders that he knew would result in the loss of life, but his orders were to hit the beaches and advance.

When the first of the Sixth Army's two hundred thousand troops landed on January 9 at Lingayen Gulf, 120 miles north of Manila, there was practically no resistance. The Japanese had been

MAP   103

distracted in the south and now the Japanese troops positioned in Manila were set to be snared between armies moving toward the capital from the south and north. Rumor spread through the underground that that the Japanese were planning to slaughter the thirty-seven hundred captives at Santo Tomas before abandoning the city to the Americans.

When MacArthur got to the headquarters of the First Cavalry Division at Guimba, one hundred miles north of Manila, on January 31, he gave startling orders to the division's commander, Maj. Gen. Verne Mudge. "Go to Manila. Go around the Japs, bounce off the Japs, save your men, but get to Manila!" he said. "Free the internees at Santo Tomas! Take Malacañan Palace and the Legislative Building."

Word spread that MacArthur wanted the former horse cavalry division to be the first US unit to enter Manila. But Beightler felt his unit deserved that honor, and had it not been for delays in repairing a bridge on the Pampanga River blown by the Japanese, he could well have made it first.

Sensing his disappointment, MacArthur draped an arm around Beightler and, as Beightler would later recall, told him that the cards were stacked against him. He thought it would be much easier for the First Cavalry, which was motorized and had seen little fighting on Luzon, to slash into the city and save the civilians at the university.

Beightler saw it as a challenge. The orders prompted something of a race between the First Cavalry Division, which was one hundred miles away, on the east flank, and the Thirty-Seventh Infantry Division, which was just twenty-five miles north of the city but on foot, on the west flank. The First Cavalry formed two flying columns and began racing to the city while avoiding large, lengthy battles with the enemy. The idea was to surprise the enemy, to push through with as many men, tanks, and artillery as quickly as possible, to stop the annihilation of all thirty-seven hundred internees at Santo Tomas. The great machines of war moved forward in the moonlight, and the Americans were greeted at each new village by crowds of Filipinos cheering and singing with hysterical fervor. They banged church bells with rocks and kissed the boys' necks and tossed flowers at their tanks.

The "Manila Derby" made sense tactically, but speed brought the danger of rushing headlong into a trap set by the Japanese Fourteenth Area Army, commanded by Gen. Tomoyuki Yamashita. And the guerrillas who had discovered the fresh mines saw what was taking shape. Thousands of soldiers would walk right into death if they didn't get the new map in time.

Joey taped the map securely between her shoulder blades, over the leprous pox that had spread to her neck and face and arms. Over that she slipped on an inconspicuous blouse, then a knapsack with shoulder straps. Her superior didn't mince the danger. "You had better go to confession and make a good act of contrition," he said, "for you will not be coming back."

They told her who to look for once she had reached the American headquarters at Calumpit, thirty-five miles north of Manila, but no one advised her how best to get there. She knew the Japanese army was spread between Manila and Calumpit, probably planning ambushes on the southbound Americans. Roads and footpaths would be guarded, and passersby would be searched, possibly stripped naked. Other dangers lurked as well, not the least of which was the Hukbalahap, the Communist guerrillas who were also fighting the Japanese but had a reputation of fighting everybody.

She went to confession and prepared herself for the long journey. Since travelers in cars were more likely to be searched, she thought it best to walk the thirty-five miles. Her illness had not subsided and she was often paralyzed by headaches and fatigue, but she swallowed her pain and set out. She walked off to the side of a two-lane highway that stretched due north out of Manila and soon reached Malolos, a little more than halfway to Calumpit, without being noticed. The Japanese sentries didn't think a little woman

MAP 105

would be going much farther, so they left her alone with perfunctory searching.

A villager in Malolos warned her of the open warfare between the Japanese and the Huks up ahead, and she decided to leave the roadway to avoid the conflicting forces. In Malolos, she hired a *banca* driver to take her along the Pampanga River to Hagonoy, but just after they left, they were pursued by six *bancas* filled with river pirates. Her *banca* was swift and the driver was unafraid and they made it to Hagonoy ahead of the pirates. She walked the remaining eight and a half miles to Calumpit but got bad news when she arrived. The Thirty-Seventh had advanced three hours earlier, relocating headquarters to Malolos. She had to turn around and walk all the way back.

When she finally found the Americans, she asked for Captain Blair, which she assumed was another alias. The soldiers subjected her to a battery of questions before letting her through. A soldier named Dixon with the 129th Infantry attached to the 37th Division passed a note through at 10:17 AM.

"A CO picked up a Filipino woman who has contact with a Capt. of the guerrilla forces," he wrote. "They have complete info of enemy installations to the South."

After much shuttling about, she was brought to Captain Blair, who put her through further questioning. Then he asked about the map. She had not spoken a word about the map, just that she was in contact with guerrillas and knew about enemy movements in the city. She removed the drawing from her back and handed it to him. The captain opened a large map that revealed all the mines and traps on the north side of Manila, including the newly sown field east of Blumentritt. He swore. Then he asked her how she slipped through Japanese lines. She told him what she had been through and he swore again.

"By God," he said. "I never dreamed that Filipino women had such courage."

She attached herself to the Thirty-Seventh and rode with the troops toward Manila in the race to be first to the city.

Other soldiers pushing north, with the help of Emmanuel de Ocampo and the Hunters, saw Manila burning from atop Tagaytay Ridge. Fires and great columns of smoke reached into the sky as the Japanese, aided by the Makapili, torched their own stores and ammo dumps. The Hunters and men from the Eleventh Airborne nonetheless pushed on before running into fierce resistance south of Nichols Field. Though they suffered some nine hundred casualties, they successfully cut the Manila Naval Defense Force's escape and sawed off reinforcement routes.

That Saturday, February 3, 1945, the First Cavalry crossed the northern city limits at 6:35 PM, a few hours before the Thirty-Seventh Division, and spread out, following MacArthur's orders to take Malacañang Palace and the Legislative Building.

The thin and hungry men, women, and children at Santo Tomas watched as American planes swooped in close, nearly buzzing the roof off the guard tower. The prisoners saw something the guards had not. From one plane a pilot dropped something that landed in a

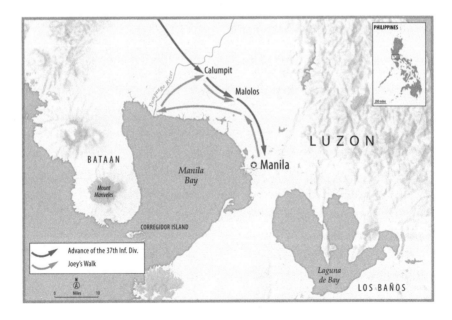

MAP   107

courtyard near the main building. One of the residents fetched the fallen object. It was a pair of goggles with a note attached. "Roll out the barrel," it said. "There'll be a hot time in the old town tonight."

When darkness fell on Santo Tomas, a great cheering could be heard filling the streets of Manila, followed by the roar of internal combustion motors and the clanking sound of metal on stone. One US Army nurse at Santo Tomas lifted her nose and said, "That smells like GI gasoline." In the confused excitement, the internees were ordered into the main building, where they listened as the rifle fire got closer and Japanese guards manned their posts. Then, a voice in the darkness:

"Where the hell is the front gate?"

Soon a tank named Battlin' Basic, from the Forty-Fourth Tank Battalion, crashed through the gates of Santo Tomas, followed by one called Georgia Peach. Capt. Manuel Colayco, a guerrilla fighter and one of Joey's friends who had led the cavalry through the city to Santo Tomas, was pointing out buildings to the Americans when, out of nowhere, a Japanese soldier lobbed a grenade. It exploded before the guerrilla, and he became the first guerilla casualty of the liberation of Manila.

The internees huddled inside one of the buildings were jarred when a soldier kicked in a door and pointed his carbine at the crowd.

"Are there any goddamned Japs in there?" he asked.

One elderly woman spoke up, tears in her eyes.

"Soldier, are you real?"

"Yes," he replied. "I reckon I am."

The soldiers were healthy white boys from places like Corning, New York, and Kerrville, Texas, and Towers Hill, Illinois, and Lewistown, Pennsylvania, and they'd all get shiny medals pinned to their uniforms for their courage and speed. The prisoners began cheering and screaming and they raced to the yard and up onto the tanks pouring in, slapping backs and crying. They sang "God Bless America" and "The Star-Spangled Banner" as soldiers cleared the buildings of the remaining Japanese guards. When one of the enemy reached for his shoulder bag, he was shot in the gut by an American major. Lieutenant Abiko, whom internees referred to as "the devil's right hand," fell on the lawn, writhing, and the crowd of internees attacked him, spitting at him and kicking him and stripping the medals from his uniform. Some slashed him with knives and others burned him with cigarettes. When they had taken their revenge, the medical staff took over and treated Abiko's wounds with sulfa and bandages, then sent him to bed, where he died within a few hours.

"War makes animals of us all," one doctor said to another.

Many Japanese soldiers had fled the city to join fighters in the mountains, but those left behind were operating under confused orders. Some holed up, prepared to fight to the death, which would prove tragic for the Filipinos and their beloved city.

General MacArthur's intelligence units weren't able to come up with a clear picture of Japanese intentions, but it seemed likely that General Yamashita would abandon the city, as MacArthur had done before. However, Manila was also being defended by a rear admiral in the Japanese navy whose duty was to destroy all naval installations. Rear Adm. Sanji Iwabuchi had already been embarrassed by MacArthur when he failed to stop the US advance along the northern coast in New Guinea. He didn't want to go down again without a fight. Yamashita disagreed with Iwabuchi, but he couldn't control the naval officer, who wanted to defend the fifteen square miles of the city to the death.

When the Thirty-Seventh entered the city, Captain Blair gave Joey permission to go anywhere, even to the front lines.

The city was in the throes of destruction. In Tondo, Japanese soldiers dragged civilians by the dozen, children included, into the Paco Lumber Yard and bayoneted them, slashed their throats, or shot them cold. The Thirty-Seventh Division found more than one hundred dead, left to rot in the heat of the sun or doused with gasoline and burned. The imperial soldiers strung dynamite in the private buildings, and as fire reached each new charge, massive explosions shook the neighborhoods and fountains of flame flicked the sky.

MAP   109

Brick and stone rained down like a hailstorm. When the Thirty-Seventh reached the camp at Bilibid Prison, they found 1,275 prisoners of war, their dirty toes sticking out of busted shoes and their mouths gaping at how large and healthy their rescuers appeared, as though they were giants or immortals. During the assault to take the prison, some of the internees were so scared they'd be slaughtered that they had tried to dig foxholes with their fingers. When the Americans tried to escort the prisoners to safety, they ran into the sniper fire that seemed to be coming from all directions.

And there in the thick of the madness was Joey, walking through the growing inferno as Japanese soldiers blew their own munitions houses, just as the Americans had done three years before. She walked through the roar of war like an angel of mercy, unafraid, bullets biting the ground at her feet. American soldiers, huddled behind walls or crouched in foxholes, marveled as she walked upright while bombs burst around her.

"You are tired," she would say to the soldiers. "Stay here and rest."

At Santo Tomas, still being targeted by Japanese potshots, twenty-two people were killed and thirty-nine were wounded on the very day General MacArthur claimed that Manila had fallen like a ripe plum. Maybe strategically, but the battle was far from over.

As the fight spun on, Joey bound up the wounds of soldiers and civilians and carried frightened children to safety. She prayed for the dying and closed the eyes of the dead. Some men she buried. She worked herself to exhaustion and was thrilled the day she suffered a hemorrhage of the lungs, thinking that soon she might die and be with God. One priest who observed her work overheard a man say, "I have not seen a human being like Joey."

Her countrymen were falling. Japanese commanders issued a special order declaring open season on Filipino civilians.

"The Americans who have penetrated into Manila have about 1,000 troops, and there are several thousand Filipino guerrillas. Even women and children have become guerrillas," it said in Japanese. "All people on the battlefield with the exception of Japanese military personnel, Japanese civilians, Special Construction Units, will be put to death."

All the Filipino men inside the walled city of Intramuros, some three thousand of them, were herded into a cell at Fort Santiago, doused with gasoline, then shot by a cannon placed 110 yards away. One witness said just fifty of the three thousand were able to escape. When American shells began falling on private homes in Ermita, the Japanese tricked residents into gathering in the plaza; then they sorted the young girls from the rest. Girls ages fifteen to twenty-five were taken to a café, where they were raped by marines coming off their shifts. One young girl was cut open by a bayonet. Another girl would later testify at a war crimes trial that she was raped by as many as fifteen men that first night.

A radioman from CBS News sent a report back to America on February 9, a full week after he had arrived at Santo Tomas with the First Cavalry.

"The fight for the city is progressing, but that progress is slow, because it is necessary to pry these suicidal maniacs out of their every hiding place, one by one and group by group," he said. "They are not trying to retreat, withdraw, or reinforce. They are just staying put until such time as we kill them off. And their ultimate death will have served but one purpose—the reduction of the population of an over-crowded Japan. Militarily it will have contributed absolutely nothing to the fast crumbling New Order of East Asia."

The Japanese, or at least some rogue elements, intended to defend Manila, and they eventually withdrew to the confines of Intramuros, entirely surrounded by sixteenth-century walls as thick as they were tall. No one was sure how many Japanese troops were inside, but they were there, firing on any fraction of exposed flesh. The radioman for CBS News, William Dunn, watched Intramuros from high atop a burned-out hotel on the opposite side of the Pasig River as a full corps, the Fourteenth, under the leadership of

MAP III

Lt. Gen. Oscar Griswold, tried to dislodge the Japanese from the ancient district.

"I had been impressed with the naval shore bombardments at Gloucester, Leyte, and Lingayen, but none of them could compare with the artillery barrage that struck those ancient walls," he would write. "In a shore bombardment, the shells that streak overhead burst long distances inland and the cacophony, while deafening, is somewhat muted by distance. In this bombardment the shells were bursting directly in front of us, barely three hundred yards distant. The shelling started exactly at 7:00 AM and continued without pause for 90 minutes, slowly grinding holes in the ancient, resisting walls but falling far short of destroying them. In those ninety minutes our artillery, mortars, and light guns poured more than three hundred tons of steel into their target as we watched."

When the hellfire stopped, there was an eerie calm.

"Now there's nothing more I can do but sweat," Griswold told the radioman. "I've given them all I've got and they're under a higher command."

26

LOS BAÑOS

The gravediggers were exhausted. They were burying four, maybe five prisoners a day, death rates ridiculously higher than in Nazi prison camps. And the guards on the perimeter had swung their big guns around so they were now pointing inside, at the internees and at Father Fred Julien, who had just celebrated his thirty-fifth birthday, his fourth in a row as a prisoner of the Japanese army.

In the past two weeks, the Allies had freed inmates at Baguio and Camp John Hay and Old Bilibid. They'd rescued thirty-seven hundred civilians at Santo Tomas, the largest camp, where they had discovered documents that gave orders to the commandant at Los Baños, twenty-four miles away, to liquidate all internees if withdrawal became necessary.

The prisoners looked like scarecrows standing in front of their barracks before roll call as a saffron sun rose on the morning of February 23, 1945. From beyond the hills came a great rumbling.

"I wonder what that is," a Dutch priest said.

"Either the Japanese up there are running or the Americans are coming," Father Julien replied. "Whichever it is, it could be very good for us."

The planes came in low over the hills, and white clouds exploded behind them, then descended like daffodils on the wind. A smoke grenade popped in a dry rice paddy beside the camp. A grenade exploded in a bunker near the front gate. The daffodils landed, ditching their chutes and shouldering rifles. Guerrillas poured out of hiding places in the undergrowth and charged the wire, attacking the gun house where the Japanese guards, caught doing calisthenics on the ball field, had left their weapons. Tracer bullets ripped through the camp, and the priests dove to the ground, praying the rosary on hot breath.

"Spare my life, almighty God," prayed Father Julien, frozen facedown with fear.

In a blink, the shooting stopped and the paratroopers fanned out, barking instructions to the frail prisoners. *Get up. Get your shit. Let's move.*

The barracks were burning now, the paratroopers pulling prisoners toward sixty amphibious vehicles bound for Laguna de Bay, toward American lines. Planes roared overhead, targeting gun emplacements and laying down cover.

One thousand one hundred seventy-four captive sunrises. Three hours, in and out. Freedom sounded like a cluster of men peppering the paratroopers with questions, learning about Santo Tomas and the destruction in Manila and the movements on the western front.

Father Julien stepped on a scale, figuring he'd lost 20 or 30 pounds off his prewar weight of 135 pounds. The needle stopped moving at eighty-seven.

27

DISPATCHED

The weeks and months after the battle wrecked Manila were tumultuous, with every system of government in chaotic flux. Public transportation did not exist. Water and sewer lines were wrecked. There was no electricity. Forty percent of the city's one hundred bridges were destroyed, including the six over the Pasig River. The University of the Philippines and Philippine General Hospital, surrounding the Ateneo de Manila, were destroyed. The same for the government center. The Americans had left the Japanese stragglers with no escape route, so they simply holed up, recklessly, forcing the Americans to clear the city building by building, floor by floor, closet by closet. It was a fight of attrition; for every American killed, US soldiers killed seventeen Japanese. Filipino civilians were caught in the middle. For every dead American soldier, one hundred civilians lost their lives. Their bodies were stacked like cordwood around the city, bayonet wounds on their backs, missing arms and legs, and sometimes, oddly, with no noticeable injuries. It is commonly believed that more than one hundred thousand civilians died during the battle. When the number of claims submitted for the deaths of Filipinos at Japanese hands were tallied after nearly four years of war, it would exceed one million.

"The war has left behind it a world suffering from destitution and seething with discontent," read the lead editorial in the *Philip-*

Destruction at Intramuros, the walled city in Manila, in May 1945, after the Battle of Manila. *Wikimedia Commons*

pines Free Press of February 23, 1946, the first publication after four years of blackout. "The old standards of living have disappeared, swept away in the whirlwind of destruction."

Bodies were turning up bearing signs of torture. Judges were sentencing traitors and collaborators to death. Frauds in spiffy new uniforms were filing claims for back pay with the US Army, saying they had fought for the resistance and deserved their due. Some signs of normalcy were creeping back in, too, and certain sections of the city were struggling to get their beat back. You could dine and dance to the music of Tirso Cruz and his orchestra at the world-famous Manila Hotel. You could catch a business flight on one of four routes offered by Philippine Air Lines. You could finally buy a "squeak and rattle-free" six-passenger Nash 600 from the Bachrach Motor Company. But the war had razed 70 percent of utilities, 75 percent of factories, and 100 percent of the business district. Only Warsaw compared in terms of devastation.

Joey's life remained in flux. Her home in Ermita was lost. She didn't own a single beautiful thing anymore. She sought refuge where she always had, with the Jesuits, who again found a way to provide. They, too, were refugees, but they found her a little room— only eight feet by six feet—in the ruined laboratories of the Ateneo. A mortar had penetrated the roof and created a gaping hole. Water poured in when it rained, which wasn't all bad. It was all the water she could get.

The campus was full of refugees, and Joey treated them the best she knew how. She couldn't resist their appeals. The food the priests set aside for her she gave to others. Father Monaghan became aware that she was only eating one meal per day. She did the same with donated clothing, picking out the outfits she liked best and giving them away. Since Father Monaghan was her spiritual counselor, he finally forbade her to give anything away without his permission.

One day he received an urgent message about Joey. Someone had informed the military police that a leper was living on the premises and the authorities thought it best that she be segregated. The priests at the Ateneo were well aware of the national embarrassment that was the state-run leprosariums in the Philippines.

Monaghan hustled to the Ateneo and listened to Joey's story. A doctor employed in the hospital across the wall from the Ateneo had informed the police against her. He was the father of Joey's closest friend, a girl with whom she had spoken of her affliction in confidence. The American army health authorities were planning to take swift action. Father Monaghan had an idea: to get her out of the Ateneo and try to hide her in seclusion. He hurried off to find a friendly army sergeant he knew, and the man helped get Joey out of the college and into the home of the family of her friend Lulu Reyes. Lulu and Joey's other friends, now in on the secret, would not tell, but they all began working to find a long-term place for Joey to stay. The Reyes family's home was ruined, and they, too, were set to move into the Ateneo in a few days.

"Is it going to be Novaliches?" Joey asked Monaghan a few days later. "I keep repeating the word to myself. At first it had a terrible sound. By forcing myself to repeat it, I am getting used to it. It is like the taste for olives—you have to cultivate it. Who knows? I may eventually come to like the thought of Novaliches."

Meanwhile, her friends were having no luck finding a place. Monaghan told Joey that it looked as though Novaliches would be the only place she could stay if they couldn't find other housing. The next day, he drove to the outskirts of town to see the leprosarium for himself. "Such another God-and-man-forsaken place as that Novaliches leprosarium I hope to never see," he wrote later. "In the midst of a wilderness of high sawgrass lay a cluster of frame houses. The director, a good man, showed me about. The objects Stevenson called 'butt-ends of humanity' squatted on the ground or lay in bed. They were given a weekly ration of food, not half what they needed; this they cooked for themselves. They had to gather their own wood; worse than that, they had to fetch all their water—for washing, laundry, and drinking. The wards were foul; no disinfectants were provided. When the poor lepers tracked up the floor with their open sores, the filth and stench and the danger of graver contagion remained. The lepers, I learned, had become brutalized from despair and the sense of their abandonment. They stole from one another and lived in complete promiscuity. The government did not provide enough money to hire help to maintain separate establishments."

When he left, Father Monaghan was sick. He thought of Saint Ignatius's picture of a soul locked in a corrupting body and banished to a wilderness among brute beasts. What was the crime of lepers that they were still treated so inhumanly by their fellow man? And why must a pure, cultured young woman be sent to a lifelong exile in a hellhole like Novaliches? There was plenty of pity for other diseases, foundations for the study of cancer and tuberculosis, but lepers were always the outcasts from whom men fled.

The next time he saw Joey, Father Monaghan told her exactly what he had seen at Novaliches. He wanted her to know the worst and to be prepared for it. He tried to offer spiritual consolation: God must have a plan for her in a place like that. He told her that if God was taking her from all the support of society to place her among those poor, forsaken creatures, it was because he meant to replace those supports with an infinitely stronger and sweeter intimacy with himself.

"Consider," he said, "that you are going to an austere cloister, a Carmel, where Christ awaits you."

The next afternoon, he drove Joey to Novaliches. Lulu and her other friends came along. They joked and laughed the entire way. When they pulled onto the campus and Joey saw the derelict compound and the crude houses, she spoke up.

"Father," she said, "how do you like my convent?"

They ate supper with the director, then packed up to leave. Lulu and the girls kissed Joey. Father Monaghan shook her hand. Joey knelt before him and asked for a blessing. He gave it, then climbed into the car and drove away. No one spoke on the drive back to Manila. They thought about how much she had given and how little she had received in return. A hero. An outcast.

28

LEPER CAMP

It started with a letter. On August 8, 1945, Joey Guerrero sat before a typewriter at the leper colony in Novaliches and composed a meek cry for help. Conditions were so dire she felt she had no choice but to ask for charity, which, the Ateneo priests knew, went against the Filipino's nature. She addressed her letter to Marie Dachauer of Sacramento, California, whom she had heard about from a friend of a friend. Dachauer, tall and efficient and originally from Milwaukee, had retired her job as manager of the Enos department store and was on her way toward founding Friends for the Lepers, a Catholic lay organization to help leprosy victims around the world. Joey tucked the note into an envelope and sent it to America on a prayer.

> Dear Miss Marie:
> One lovely afternoon last week a young army chaplain came to an isolated part of the world with four young Jesuit scholastics. The young army chaplain was also a Jesuit. They came to visit a young woman, a very good friend of the other four young Jesuit scholastics. The place is about twenty-eight kilometers away from the city of Manila but they came in an army jeep and although the roads were all ruts and holes and rough travel, they

got there in a very short while. This out-of-the-way and almost forgotten and forsaken place is a leprosarium and the young woman they came to visit is the person who takes the liberty to write to you. The young army chaplain is Father (Captain) Luis Torralba, S.J. and the twenty-eight year old young woman is called Joey—Joey to all her friends and hopes that in time you might be one amongst them and that she be Joey to you also.

And now that I have (I hope) properly introduced myself, may I say that Father has spoken so highly of you and thinks you are a very wonderful person. He said I may write and so I have. I do hope you will not think this an intrusion, nay, an imposition on the goodness and greatness of your heart which Father has told us about. However, I took courage to do so for he spoke of your great interest and devotion to the needs and fate of the leper.

Someday I hope you may come to the Philippines and perhaps pay us a visit, but in the meantime, I'd like to tell you all about us. May I? Father says I must tell you everything. But the inside story of the life of the leper in a poor and sadly abandoned leper colony is too full of heartaches, misery and want. I always argued and thought that to dump our many troubles and vicissitudes on the laps of other people very inconsiderate and unfair: and many are the times when I feel that it is truly an imposition to ask even my own friends out here into this no-man's land of a leper colony but my little girl's heart always wins out by the thought that this is what my friends are for; that I may turn to them in times of stress, that I may unburden to them the weight of the cross that lies heavy at times in my heart.

First I want you to know that I am happy to suffer in God's love. . . . For what joy can be greater? It would

not be human if I were to tell you that I am never otherwise for that would not be true. There are moments
of unspeakable loneliness, of unexplained longings and
yearnings and too many contretemps in which one's heart
is tried to the core. But I feel that our Lord desires this
strange hidden life for me for reasons I shall never know
until He calls me Home. So I have made my oblation and
only ask that He give me grace and strength enough to
follow His will. I look forward to heaven and the thought
keeps me forever joyous and young in heart.

But my companions are not so easily led like children
as I am and are, I am afraid, grown bitter or despairing,
futile or helpless, depraved or hateful. The rest are simply apathetic or cynically indifferent. The moral, physical,
and spiritual degradation will bring a sob to your throat.
I desire so much to be able to alleviate all this human
misery, and wish, at least, to instill once more the feeling
of hope and make their lives once more wholesome and
brighter. But I am only one of them segregated and isolated, of myself, I can really do nothing. I need your help.
Perhaps you will be our fairy godmother and with your
magic wand help to make the leper's life less despairing,
less miserable and ease the sense of futility in his heart.
How wonderful that would be for us lepers! God bless
you and love you Miss Marie, for your kind understanding and sympathy.

There used to be over six hundred lepers here, but
during the Japanese regime, several hundred died of starvation or malnutrition. There are only ninety of us here
right now. However, two hundred and fifty some are
arriving sometime at the end of the month. The place
will be overcrowded. As it is there are only ten run-down
cottages, all leaks and broken shutters and one great long-
ish building divided into two which serves as infirmaries

for the very sick and bed-ridden. All of the roofs need repairs, for more often than not, the rains come and the rotting wooden flooring is flooded and the poor, helpless patients get all huddled in one corner to escape getting drenched. There isn't a single decent bed. All of them are dirty, rusty, and sagging in all places, rickety and there isn't one thing that is not run down. The whole place is a disgrace.

Malaria abounds in this region and mosquito nets are truly a necessity. However the patients are so poor, most of them have neither decent mosquito netting, pillow, bed linen. . . . In fact, most of them are in rags. Food is terribly insufficient, but I guess this can be remedied as soon as things get to normal, or will it?

Medicine? Even that is not adequate. We have no laboratories here, we have not sufficient medical help, we have no complete medical instruments. . . . In short this is not a hospital. . . . It is a prison for the patients classed no better than common criminals.

Why does science, medical science, do everything for other diseases? Other hospitals have practically every necessity for their patients but the leper, as usual, gets the raw side. All the others must have this, must have that, but the leper can wait. Usually he waits in vain. They say the government is poor, yet it has funds for everything else otherwise. Why? Is it because the world has conspired against the leper? Because, once a leper, always a leper?

But I am being furious for nothing perhaps. I suppose the lot of the leper is like this. Or is it? Or should it be? Then, I want to do something about it. The administration thinks the leper is cursed . . . he is a hopeless element. Is the leper utterly to be blamed if he has learned to take the law in his hands, has become rebellious, covetous, nay, almost repulsive in his sense of values? Living here, I have learned that perhaps the blame does not lie wholly on the leper himself. . . . The world should stop by for a few moments from its fast and turbulent pace and give the leper a passing glance. But the world has gone all smug and materialistic and the leper has become as a-grain-of-sand-in-a-mighty-ocean in insignificance . . . no one remembers that he exists. Yet, he is as human as anybody's next door neighbor and he is starved for solicitude and affection. Most of us here are completely abandoned and forsaken by our own families . . . the rest have no one.

We have no lights, no water, nothing to amuse us by way of recreation. I have tried to get us all together every Sunday afternoon to sing and tell stories. I have been begging from friends for a guitar, a ukulele, a mandolin, and a banjo, so we can make some music . . . we have nothing as yet. I'd like us to have a radio with phonograph and records (popular and classical music). . . . I have been begging for game sets like chess, ping-pong, badminton, volley ball, basket ball, backgammon, checkers, etc., books to read, comics, papers. . . . Oh Miss Marie, if you could see how hungry my lepers are for these things . . . poor ones, all they have is an old, out-of-tune harmonica. . . . Please wave your magic wand and send us at least a guitar and a set of dominoes to play with and if your magic wand can work wonders and produce most of these things, all we can do is say "thank you" from the bottom of our hearts. We shall never be able to repay you in this world, but Our Lord is never outdone in generosity . . . we can only keep you in our prayers. I shall keep you always in mine.

I am afraid I have tired you with this dull monologue of our petty troubles and wants, but we are in need of a true friend. I was assured that you would be and if I have imposed on your charity, I beg that you understand and forgive my audacity. I am a little girl at heart . . . I have only spoken in utter disregard to Miss Emily Post. . . . I'm afraid I have no conventions. I say what I want and feel . . . please excuse me.

Some day soon I hope you will come to our lovely country, no longer very lovely because of the ravages of war, but the countryside is still verdant and green after the rains . . . some of it is still very lovely anyway. We look forward to better times.

My own home with everything in it is gone up in smoke and the few pieces of clothes I have are generous gifts from friends. I have lost the little I have but no matter . . . some of us in this crazy world are asked to offer some sacrifice. But our good God sustains us in all our troubles and vicissitudes and He makes us suffer according to our ability to bear them without losing patience or faith. He knows the destiny of our souls as it were.

And now really I mustn't go on tiring you this way. Please write, won't you and tell me all about your work and yourself. I hope my narrative hasn't made your heart heavy . . . I have not meant to be inconsiderate.

Goodbye then and our Lord bless you and keep you.

As ever sincerely in the Hearts of Jesus and Mary,

Joey Guerrero

When Marie Dachauer received the letter, she forwarded it to Father Abbot Paul at the only US leprosarium, in a little backwater town called Carville, Louisiana. Father Paul in turn passed it along to Ann Page, a patient at Carville who was on the staff of the patient newsletter, the *Star*, which had an impressive nationwide circulation and emblazoned its mission on the masthead of every issue: *Radiating the Light of Truth on Hansen's Disease*. Ann Page wasted no time in sharing the letter with her friends at Carville, who began to organize a drive to deliver clothes, linens, and games to their peers on the other side of the earth.

"We felt we had to help," Page would say.

The patients came forward with apparel, games, books, and magazines. The Filipino patients paid the shipping charges on the first boxes.

Page wrote back to Dachauer, asking for Joey's address so they could send the goods. Then she wrote to Joey directly, being careful not to sound pitiful. As desperate as Joey's situation sounded, Page knew there were promising discoveries being made in the treatment of leprosy, and most of them were happening right there at Carville.

November 5, 1945

Dear Joey,

Miss Marie Dachauer of Sacramento, Calif., has sent a copy of your letter to our resident Catholic Chaplain, Father Abbot Paul who in turn has furnished us with a copy of it. We read it with a great deal of interest as we, patients of the National Leprosarium, are deeply interested in victims of Hansen's disease all over the world. Your address was not on the letter so I am writing to Miss Dachauer and enclosing this letter to you with the request that she send it on to you.

I am known in Carville as Ann Page. I have been here for a number of years and am employed as the school teacher and librarian. *The Star* is our monthly magazine, printed and edited entirely by patients. As soon as you furnish us with a more complete mailing address we want to send it to you regularly so that you can be posted on everything that is going on here and all that we know about the new drugs.

We also wish to send some games and books to the patients at your hospital. We have more than we need of these things and it is a pleasure to share them with you good folks. Our Medical Officer in Charge has consented to our sending these things to you. We are constantly trying to contact English speaking patients and to bring patients of different colonies into correspondence with each other. We feel that all of us have a mutual bond and that we are better off for being in touch with each other. Is it difficult to get things mailed to your hospital? By that I mean is there a regular system of mail delivery. We receive our mail daily here but you spoke of the inaccessibility of your home and the terrible roads to it.

Diasone is used here on a number of patients. Those patients able to tolerate it seem to respond. Streptomycin is not used because there is not enough of it available to even supply the needs of the armed forces. Promin is given to some 125 of us by daily intravenous injections. They have been using this for something over 4 years and it definitely has been beneficial. The health of the average patient now is far better than it had been before the Promin treatment. With both Promin and Diasone the blood count must be watched closely. We are given blood counts every third week. The red blood cells are prone to be broken down and to avoid this we are constantly given vitamins. If our blood does drop we are taken off of the shots until it rebuilds. This has been wonderful in preventing total blindness where it has been given soon enough. For acute red eyes penicillin is given in large doses for a couple of days and where the pain used to continue for months now it is over in a day or two. Victims of Hansen's disease must take courage now for while we have had the treatment already it will come to each and every one of you.

Mr. Perry Burgess, President of the Leonard Wood Memorial, will leave for Manila this month. He is being sent a copy of your letter and we are asking him to look you up and see what can be done for you people in a medical way at least. Housing, etc. will, I assume, have to be taken care of by your government.

Do let us hear from you, Joey, and remember to tell the patients to take heart for our lot is not the black picture it once was—science is rapidly moving forward in our behalf.

Our best wishes to you and your fellow patients.

Anne Page

The same day, Page wrote to Perry Burgess, whose offices were at 1 Madison Avenue in New York. Burgess's organization had been named after Leonard Wood, an American soldier who had served as governor general in the Philippines and greatly promoted the cause of the leper, spending nearly a third of the total public health budget in the islands trying to eradicate the disease. A decade after Wood's death in 1927, Burgess had written a book that told the story of an American soldier in a Philippine leper colony, and he made regular trips to visit colonies in the Philippines.

"From Joey's letter you can readily see that these people are desperately in need of help and we feel that the Leonard Wood Memorial can be of assistance, providing for some of their immediate physical needs," Page wrote. "We hope that you will have the opportunity of personally visiting the particular place and we would like to have a first-hand report from you concerning conditions there. We realize, of course, that the entire Philippine set-up is in a deplorable post-war state."

She informed him that packages weighing up to seventy pounds, if marked "Chaplain Supplies," could be sent to the Philippines. Marie Dachauer was collecting mosquito netting, and Betty Martin, another patient at Carville, was trying to get her hands on musical instruments and books and magazines. Page apologized for being a burden and asked Burgess if he could lend a hand as well.

Burgess went to Tala, in Novaliches, to visit Joey the following week and reported back to Page and the Carville patients that all was as bad if not worse than Joey had said and that Joey herself was a "lovely, cultured person."

Soon Page heard directly from Joey, who still sounded in shock that a modern country, no matter how war-torn, would leave its most vulnerable cases in such awful conditions.

"During the Japanese regime and during the liberation, the horror, the massacre, the unspeakable devastation and ruin are beyond comprehension," she wrote. "Then I came here to stay to find sick, crippled, starving people lying on pallets, pieces of straw on the floor, everything a filthy mess, the patients moving around like skeletons on strings, bundled or hardly covered with clothing, eating cats and dogs. When I saw these things it took every vestige of courage and stamina I had. I felt like just leaving the place in a great hurry. I have never seen a case of leprosy, except my own, until I went to Novaliches. You must know how I felt. Now everything is different because they all depend on me like little children. I have found great peace and happiness in this forced exile and everything about me has taught me to be a better person. I have become tolerant and understanding of others."

Joey was working as a schoolteacher for the children at Novaliches, on top of ministering to the sick and burying the dead. The aid from Marie Dachauer and Ann Page and the patients at Carville, while helpful, had only lasted a short while. Joey's next appeal was to the Bureau of Health for medicine, but she was told they had no money.

There was one more option.

29

LOOSE ENDS

On February 23, 1946, a year to the day after the raid to free the starving prisoners at Los Baños, flood lights shone on the thirteen steps leading up to the black gallows not far from the camp. It was 3:00 AM. The predawn stars looked like little pinpricks of light in the tropical sky.

Gen. Tomoyuki Yamashita, Tiger of Malaya, climbed the steps without emotion, his hands bound together in front. A wire fence twenty-five feet high surrounded the gallows, and it was covered with camouflage netting. The newspaper reporters and photographers were barred from the area. A heavily armed guard patrolled the perimeter. A Japanese priest accompanied the defeated general, who was dressed in American khaki trousers and shirt and wearing a green fatigue hat. He had been stripped of his medals on orders from MacArthur.

Lt. Charles Rexroad, of Corvallis, Oregon, an ex–football player who stood six foot three and weighed 245 pounds and would tally 130 executions before the war was over, stepped aside and directed the paunchy Gen. Tomoyuki Yamashita to his place and slid a Manila hemp rope around his neck. Rexroad, the son of a Methodist minister, would later say he chose the length of the rope based on the scope of the atrocities and that he never lost a wink of sleep about it. In fact, he had been eligible for discharge, but he stayed in the Philippines for this execution in particular, not for the $200 bonus he was to receive.

If the stories belong to the victors, the Japanese general's end was an integral piece of Douglas MacArthur's narrative. After he liberated Manila at a heavy cost, MacArthur deployed the Eighth Army in great stinging maneuvers that caught the Japanese by surprise throughout the islands, cutting them off from supplies, trapping them, chasing them into the mountains, where the guerrillas ambushed them. Without the permission of his superiors, MacArthur vanquished the enemy in the Philippines with speed, dash, and brilliance. After the fighting on Luzon, he lost just 820 soldiers to the 21,000 Japanese killed in action. "The Japanese during the operations employed twenty-three divisions, all of which were practically annihilated," he announced in July 1945. "Our forces comprised seventeen divisions. This was one of the rare instances when in a long campaign a ground force superior in numbers was entirely destroyed by a numerically inferior opponent." With Adolf Hitler's suicide in April and Germany's surrender in May, the Soviets joined the Allies in the fight in the Pacific. American troops who had been slugging it out in Europe were sent to help the general mop up and, if the emperor refused to capitulate, invade the Japanese homeland. Such an invasion seemed imminent by late June when the United States won the Battle of Okinawa, where 110,549 Japanese died. Japan's best warships were at the bottom of the ocean. The United States had air bases on Iwo Jima and Saipan and firebombed city after city. An estimated 267,000 buildings in Tokyo alone burned to the ground. Bomber crews returned with the stench of burning flesh in their nostrils, a smell some of them would remember decades later, on their deathbeds.

On August 6, a B-29 bomber called the *Enola Gay* dropped a nine-thousand-pound atomic bomb called Little Boy on the Japanese manufacturing city of Hiroshima. President Harry Truman, who had assumed office after Roosevelt's death on April 12, 1945, said: "If they do not now accept our terms, they may expect a rain of ruin from the air, the like of which has never been seen on this earth. Behind this air attack will follow sea and land forces in such numbers and power as they have not yet seen and with the fighting skill of which they are already well aware." On August 8, the Soviets invaded Japanese-occupied Manchuria by land. On August 9, another B-29, this one called *Bockscar*, dropped an even larger atomic bomb called Fat Man on the Japanese city of Nagasaki.

The combined bombs killed some two hundred thousand Japanese civilians, many of whom believed that the home islands, now burning and blasted to hell, were sacred, that they'd formed from salty drops of water that fell from the halberd that belonged to a god, and that Japan would ultimately win the war.

Finally, on August 15, Emperor Hirohito ordered an end to hostilities. Japan sent sixteen delegates to Manila to negotiate terms of surrender plans. When those were settled on, MacArthur flew to the battered country in his C-54, with BATAAN painted on its nose. His staff was wary of a trap or of an attack from a remaining fanatic band of soldiers who refused to follow their emperor's orders. They remembered Pearl Harbor and Manila. But MacArthur told them to stand down, to disarm, that nothing would impress the conquered like a show of absolute fearlessness. Upon arrival at the New Grand Hotel in Yokohama, MacArthur even refused to let someone else taste his steak for poison.

His second dinner at the hotel was interrupted when it was announced he had a visitor. MacArthur was headed for the lobby when the door swung open. There stood his old friend, Gen. Jonathan Wainwright, whom he had left on Corregidor with the command to never surrender. Wainwright, leaning on a cane, was a shadow of his former self. His eyes were sunken, his hair white, his face like shoe leather. He'd been freed from a Japanese prison camp, where he'd been held captive for three years, three months, and eighteen days. He was fed little and was forced to bow to abusive prison guards. He was allowed no outside news, so he spent long days wondering how the war was going and what the nation thought about the general who surrendered the Philippines, if they thought about him at all. He wondered what MacArthur felt, too.

Wainwright would be pinned with the Medal of Honor by President Truman and grace the cover of *Time* magazine and receive a hero's welcome in a ticker tape parade through New York City. But in that moment all he could manage in his shame was one word.

"General . . ." Wainwright said, then burst into tears.

"Why, Jim," MacArthur said, using Wainwright's private nickname. "Your old corps is yours when you want it."

Wainwright was further humbled and, to the reporters gathered, he modestly expressed his "heartfelt gratitude" to the American people "for their generous understanding of my dire misfortune when I was forced by circumstances beyond my control to surrender to the Japanese forces at Corregidor.

"The belief that you appreciated the difficulties of my position has sustained and comforted me during the years of my captivity, and I thank you, all of you, for your generosity."

Two days later, on September 2, a Sunday morning, Wainwright climbed the starboard ladder to the deck of the huge battleship USS *Missouri*, the likes of which he had never before seen. An admiral showed him where to stand for the ceremony, in a place of honor, flanking MacArthur. Overhead flew the American flag that had flown over the Capitol in Washington on December 7, 1941. Wainwright listened as MacArthur addressed the Allied commanders—the Canadians, New Zealanders, Australians, Chinese, Russians, French, Brits, and Dutch—and the Japanese dignitaries and foreign ministers before him. He wore no medals, just five small gold stars on his collar. "We are gathered here, representatives of the major warring powers—to conclude a solemn agreement whereby peace may be restored. The issues involving divergent ideals and ideologies have been determined on the battlefields of the world and hence are not for our discussion or debate. Nor is it for us here to meet, representing as we do a majority of the people of the earth, in a spirit of distrust, malice or hatred. But rather it is for us, both victors and vanquished, to rise to that higher dignity which alone befits the sacred purposes we are about to serve, committing all our people unreservedly to faithful compliance with the obligation they are here formally to assume," he said. "It is my earnest hope and indeed the hope of all mankind that from this solemn occasion a better world shall emerge out of the blood and carnage of the past—a world founded upon faith and understanding—a world dedicated to the dignity of man and the fulfillment of his most cherished wish—for freedom, tolerance, and justice."

One thunderstruck Japanese diplomat would say the general's words sailed on wings: "For the living heroes and dead martyrs of the war this speech was a wreath of undying flowers."

MacArthur then invited the Japanese commanders and diplomats to sign the surrender documents, which the army had printed on rare parchment paper found in a basement in devastated Manila.

Gen. Douglas MacArthur during formal surrender ceremonies on the USS *Missouri* in Tokyo Bay on September 2, 1945. Behind General MacArthur are Lt. Gen. Jonathan Wainwright and Lt. Gen. A. E. Percival.
National Archives and Records Administration

MacArthur then signed each of the five documents with a different pen, handing the first pen to Wainwright, who saluted before
accepting. After the Allied commanders signed, the Japanese disembarked and a great mass of planes, American B-29s, came in from
the south, flown by the same boys who had firebombed the Japanese cities, boys who would be home to Oklahoma or Arkansas or
Nevada in time for Thanksgiving dinner. They dropped no bombs
this time but banked in a sweeping turn and disappeared toward
the distant Mount Fuji.

MacArthur then addressed the American people by radio. The
Japanese diplomats in the gun room of the destroyer on its way
back to port heard the address as well. MacArthur's wife, Jean, also
listened from Manila.

"Today the guns are silent. A great tragedy has ended. A great
victory has been won. The skies no longer rain death—the seas bear
only commerce. Men everywhere walk upright in the sunlight.
The entire world is quietly at peace. The holy mission has been
completed. And in reporting this to you, the people, I speak for
the thousands of silent lips, forever stilled among the jungles and
the beaches and in the deep waters of the Pacific which marked
the way. I speak for the unnamed brave millions homeward bound
to take up the challenge of that future which they did so much to
salvage from the brink of disaster."

He spoke of the energy of the Japanese and of his desire for the
empire, with the right guidance, to expand upward instead of outward. He pointed to the Philippines as an example.

"In the Philippines, America has evolved a model for this new
free world of Asia," he said. "In the Philippines, America has demonstrated that peoples of the East and peoples of the West may walk
side by side in mutual respect and with mutual benefit. The history
of our sovereignty there has now the full confidence of the East."

There remained the matter of accepting the surrender of Japanese outliers in the Philippines, and MacArthur put Lt. Gen.
Wilhelm Styer, commander of US forces in the western Pacific, in

American planes fly in formation during surrender ceremonies aboard
the USS *Missouri* near Tokyo, Japan, on September 2, 1945.
National Archives and Records Administration

charge. The next day, Styer and Wainwright flew to Manila. What
was left of the Japanese armed forces continued to fight until many
of them heard the emperor's surrender by radio and turned themselves in. The largest group of holdouts on Luzon, some forty thousand sick and wounded soldiers, were loosely organized around
Kiangan, northeast of Baguio, an area that had come to be known
as Yamashita's Pocket. Yamashita was still commanding troops as
he awaited word of the official surrender signing in Tokyo. Once
that was confirmed, Yamashita, wearing a patched uniform and his
ancestor's seven-hundred-year-old sword, turned himself in to an
American delegation and was flown to Baguio to meet Styer and
Wainwright.

The tables had turned. Japan's Greater East Asia bubble had
burst. "I am without words to tell the thrill of seeing the surrender

aboard the *Missouri*," Wainwright said, "and I have an equal thrill just now seeing the imperial command bow and bend to the United States. During the first five months of this war, we were handled rather severely and lacked the force to combat these people. The shoe is on the other foot today."

A Japanese army of nearly half a million soldiers had been vanquished. Yamashita signed the surrender documents, officially ending the fighting in the Philippines. Once word spread, other commanders followed suit. Four thousand troops in Davao Province capitulated, then twenty-nine hundred on Cebu, fourteen hundred on Negros, two thousand in the Agusan Valley. Yamashita was flown directly to Manila, then to New Bilibid Prison, and placed in white-washed cell no. 1, where he was held until he was tried by a military commission for failing to prevent war crimes. He meekly argued through an interpreter that he was nothing more than a soldier at war with the task of killing those trying to kill him.

At his trial, a woman testified to seeing a Japanese soldier hold a fifteen-year-old girl's head up by her hair and hack at her neck with a sword as she prayed for mercy. Others told the commission that Japanese soldiers put candy and whiskey in the center of a college dining hall where eight hundred people were imprisoned, and as the curious crowd drew near, they set off explosives, killing hundreds. Witnesses said troops rounded up thousands of women and girls, chose the prettiest, and led them off to Manila hotels to be raped. Some were only twelve years old.

Eleven-year-old Rosalinda Andoy, who parted her straight black hair on the side and wore a pink dress and sandals, spoke in Tagalog about the day Japanese soldiers began setting fire to homes in Intramuros, and told how her parents had fled with her down smoke-choked streets to the safety of a cathedral. But the soldiers came there, too, she said, and snatched her father away to Fort Santiago, where he was killed. As Yamashita stared blankly at the table before him, the girl in the pink dress told the court how more soldiers came and lobbed grenades amid the women and children in the church, then began stabbing survivors with their bayonets. She showed the five US generals on the commission ten scars on her left arm, four more on her right. She lifted her pink dress to show them five scars on her legs, eighteen on her chest and stomach, one on her back. She told them her mother's last words were "Always to be good." She said she stayed with her mother's body until dawn; then the war's newest orphan crawled away, her intestine bulging from one of the wounds, to some nuns in a convent.

Despite the stirring testimony, there was little justice in his trial. The tribunal consisted of regular army officers who were answerable to MacArthur. They entertained much hearsay and conjecture, and the court itself determined the credibility of the witnesses. Twelve reporters who had sat through the entire trial polled each other and found Yamashita innocent, twelve to zero. One of Yamashita's lawyers said that "no American who loves his country can read the record of the prosecution's efforts in this respect without an abiding and painful sense of shame." The US Supreme Court upheld the conviction, but writing for the dissent, Justice Frank Murphy said that the "spirit of revenge and retribution, masked in formal legal procedure for purposes of dealing with a fallen enemy commander, can do more lasting harm than all of the atrocities giving rise to that spirit. . . . Today the lives of Yamashita and Homma, leaders of enemy forces vanquished on the field of battle, are taken without regard to the due process of law."

It mattered not.

Now the stocky general, six feet tall and two hundred pounds, stood on the black gallows in a sugarcane field outside Los Baños with a noose around his neck. He had offered a statement before his sentencing, and some of those present wondered if the calm and stoic man before them felt now how he had then.

"I wish to state that I stand here today with clear conscience," he had said. "I want to thank the United States of America for a fair trial. I swear before my Creator that I am innocent of the charges brought against me."

Lt. Charles Rexroad readied the lever to spring the trapdoor beneath Yamashita's feet. Yamashita asked for permission to bow to the emperor. Permission was granted, but he couldn't orient himself, so he asked the guard which direction Tokyo was. The GI indicated, and the general bowed. The GI would tell his buddies later that he didn't know whether he pointed north, south, or toward China.

"I will pray for the emperor's long life," Yamashita said quietly, "and his prosperity forever."

The Tiger of Malaya fell through the floor, a sudden heave of gravity, and dangled there in the floodlights under a blanket of tropical stars, a few hours short of another sunrise.

30

VISITS

The rebuilding of Manila came slow but steady, and soon the bridges and roads were being repaired, and soon, on hot afternoons, Renato Guerrero was loading Cynthia in his car for the long drive to Tala, Novaliches, where Joey was doing her best to care for her fellow inmates. The drive was only twenty or so miles from Manila, through the guava trees and saw-grass fields, but the roads were horrible and the village felt so far removed from the city, so isolated.

Cynthia was still in elementary school, but she was slim and her mother thought she was destined to be tall. During their infrequent visits, Joey could tell their relationship had already grown strained. Cynthia was quiet, uncommunicative, aloof even. She always seemed to be deep in thought, but she would sometimes open up as she would with a friend and the two would talk about her other friends at school, what they liked to do and what their latest hobbies were.

Joey noticed that Cynthia was full of unpredictable humor. The daughter commonly called her mother "my pinup girl."

When another patient asked Cynthia if Joey was her mother, she responded, "Who? This girl? She is my sister." On another occasion, after Joey's name and photograph were in the newspaper several days in a row, Cynthia said, "See this? The girl of the headlines!"

Cynthia would remember the visits for the rest of her life, remember how her mother was always in good spirits, even if Cynthia could tell she was physically sick. Her mother had managed to get a room of her own, and it was by then filling with books. Joey loved to read and shelved any book she could get her hands on. She helped other inmates at Tala Leprosarium as well, including a leprosy victim who had given birth. The baby girl was healthy and did not have the disease. Joey became so attached that she pulled her husband aside one day and made a bold suggestion. He should adopt the child.

Renato eventually agreed, and they took the baby into their home. Cynthia, who was being raised in large part by her father and grandmother, now had a sister, Jennifer.

Renato did not explain much to Cynthia about her mother's illness, just that she was sick and had to be isolated. The ignorance didn't assuage the sadness Cynthia felt. She missed her mother. The visits were never long enough. Her father cried for her. He wasn't expecting a miracle, but he was aware of the recent success of new drugs, still elusive in postwar Manila.

Joey, meanwhile, was trying to bring attention to the abysmal conditions at the leprosarium. "There was no medicine. The cottages were filthy," she would later say. "I was sick in my stomach. But I couldn't sit around and do nothing about it."

Joey won the confidence of the other patients at Tala. Then she started cleaning. She scrubbed the floors and disinfected the sinks. She enlisted the aid of women she knew on the outside. She wrote more letters to new friends in the United States. The patients at Carville sent as much as they could.

She appealed to the United Nations Relief and Rehabilitation Administration, which promised to set up running water and electricity.

She was shocked to learn that when patients died, they weren't buried in coffins. The other patients didn't have the spirit or energy to build a coffin, so Joey did it herself. It was a crude thing and not well constructed, but it was a solid box.

Rev. Calvert Alexander, editor of a publication called *Jesuit Missions*, was on an around-the-world trip to visit all Jesuit establishments when he stopped at Tala. He found Joey acting as sacristan of the colony's chapel. She also served as bell ringer and catechist, and when priests were unable to come in time, she baptized the dying and read the burial prayers at their graves. Alexander sent a dispatch to the National Catholic Welfare Council news service, describing Joey as "the most colorful and unforgettable character in post-war Philippines." He wrote that she lived by a simple doctrine: "Our Lord suffered, so did Our Lady and all the saints; we must do the same, gaily and joyfully, if we want to make a worthwhile contribution to our fellow men and to our peace and happiness."

She appealed to a friend and former schoolmate, Maria Aurora "Baby" Quezon, daughter of the former president Manuel Quezon. The two leaned on friends at the *Manila Times*, and eventually a newspaperman agreed to take a trip with Quezon to Tala, to see for himself. It wasn't long before the whole country would know Tala's secret.

31

IN SICKNESS

In May 1946, Gertrude Hornbostel, who had been held captive at the Santo Tomas Internment Camp for three long years, began to notice slight numbness of the hands and strange blemishes on her arms, legs, and body. She learned she had Hansen's disease in San Francisco. She was placed in an isolation ward at Letterman General Hospital but had one constant visitor, her husband, Maj. Hans Hornbostel.

The tall, broad-shouldered man wouldn't leave his wife's side, and when medical authorities decided to ship Gertrude to the nation's leprosarium at Carville for treatment, Hans decided he would go, too. His résumé lent a certain surety to his decision. The major had been serving with an army demolition squad when the Japanese overran the Philippines four years before, and he had been captured on Bataan. He survived the death march and was imprisoned for the remainder of the war in a POW camp in Cabanatuan, sixty-five miles north of where his wife was interned. Finally reunited, he wasn't about to leave her side.

Their story, and his persistence to live the rest of his years with the woman he loved, made national news. The headlines were sensational. Newspapers couldn't resist the shock value of the word *leper*, still in use for the "dread disease." The San Francisco *Call-Bulletin* broke the story, headlined S.F. WIFE LEPER: ARMY MATE

BEGS TO SHARE ISOLATION FOR LIFE. Major Hornbostel made no secret of his wife's affliction, which was a rare departure. Most patients at Carville even registered under fake names so their families wouldn't face repercussions from the ignorant. Those at Carville knew that great strides had been made in research and that doctors were finding major success with sulfone drugs, in use for six years by then. They despised the way in which many in the press continued to view leprosy, epitomized by a well-intentioned editorial in the Springfield (MA) *Union* a few days after the Hornbostel story broke on the other coast.

> For centuries this loathsome and dreadful disease has rendered its victims outcasts and untouchables. Major Hornbostel is ready to leave the outside world with its accustomed comforts, its safety, its cleanliness behind him to enter that dark place which brings to mind that ominous word "unclean." To be with his wife, he is ready to run the risk himself becoming a leper. If this man is allowed to join his wife, he will bring the colony of the doomed a luminous spirit of love and sacrifice which will not only help make existence happier for his life's companion, but also give some measure of inspiration to the other victims.

Doomed. Dark. Unclean.

The Hornbostels knew better. Gertrude called the poppycock a "melodramatic mess." In fifty-two years of the Carville hospital's existence, there had never been a known case of transmission to a doctor or nurse. And doctors were having excellent results with three sulfa drugs: Promin, Diasone, and Promizole. The year before, the leprosarium discharged thirty-seven patients, with plans to discharge forty or more in 1946.

Dr. Guy H. Faget, medical chief at Carville, was reporting that the sulfones had "stopped even the most hopeless cases in their tracks."

On the strength of the new treatments, the newly created National Advisory Council on Leprosy was preparing recommendations for a more humane policy of treatment for victims. They were planning to encourage the US surgeon general to establish new diagnostic centers and clinics for treatment in the four states where leprosy is endemic—California, Florida, Louisiana, and Texas. They also were planning to recommend segregation as a last resort and to appeal for better facilities and more freedom for patients at Carville. Even though most of Carville's patients were dealing with advanced stages of leprosy, heavy daily injections of Promin were known to clear out the bacilli swiftly. It typically took between eighteen months and five years to suppress the disease.

But culture had been slow to change. Every state but New York required segregation of lepers. Patients at Carville were still called "inmates." Hospital staff sterilized their outgoing letters. Patients could not leave of their own free will, and family members who weren't afflicted were barred from living on the hospital campus.

Hans Hornbostel felt like his only chance to be with his wife of thirty-three years was blunt talk with reporters. Instead of treating the diagnosis as something to be kept secret, he was unafraid and unashamed. He called a press conference to plea for the right to live with his wife. He tried to correct reporters when they suggested his wife caught the disease at Santo Tomas, suggesting instead that she likely contracted it much earlier and the disease revealed itself due to malnourishment and stress.

"I don't consider myself any martyr by asking to be with her as long as we both shall live," he said. "I'd be unhappy without her and she'd be unhappy without me, and that's all there is to it."

He appealed to his friend, Gen. Douglas MacArthur, who cabled from Tokyo, "I heartily endorse your desire to be with your wife." He appealed to the US Public Health Service, which suggested he get a job at Carville to ensure he could at least visit her every day.

"I've done a lot of things in my life," Hans told reporters. "I've written stories; I've been a mine superintendent; I've been an explorer and a department head; and I've served in the army and the Marine Corps; I've been a forester and a chief of police—and I see no reason why I shouldn't be damned good at kitchen police or even a missionary."

They'd married in Guam in 1913, and the war years were the only three they'd been apart.

"He says he's had his fling in life and that he wants to be with me," Gertrude said from her hospital room, which was filled with roses. "I want him to come with me."

"I just want one thing in my life: to be with my wife," the major said. "It's not unselfish of me."

When Gertrude was transferred to Carville, her husband followed her and followed the rules without a fuss. He bought her a little cottage on the hospital campus and found himself a place not too far away, and he visited every day from 7:00 AM to 7:00 PM. Thousands of letters and telegrams poured in for Gertrude, and she answered each of them, enlightening her correspondents on Hansen's disease. She also began writing a column in the patient newsletter, which was circulated coast to coast by subscription. In her column, called As I See It, she challenged the hospital administration's policies. In one, she quoted the Hippocratic Oath: "Whatever, in connection with my professional practice, or not in connection with it, I may see or hear in the lives of men which ought not to be spoken abroad, I will not divulge, as reckoning that such should be kept secret." Then she asked:

Are doctors connected with the Public Health Service exempt from the above? Or perhaps I should say: Is the patient who is committed to this hospital beyond the pale protection which the Hippocratic Oath gives, because this is a federal institution? Should a patient's private affairs, feelings, and personal symptoms become public property, to be bandied about the grounds of this institution and in the country's press?

In the first place . . . we have no private consultation room in this hospital for monthly check-ups. When the patient wants to tell the doctor something that should be told in private, he (or she) cannot do so because . . . he is separated from the doctor's office by a chain, with the whole room behind him full of other patients who can listen in. This becomes at times embarrassing, with the result that some patients keep putting off their troubles until it is too late.

Secondly, I consider it unethical to bring press representatives to clinics without the specific consent of the patients to be interviewed, as was done in the case of the AP story of Jimmie and his family. These patients were under the impression that the man taking notes was just another doctor.

While many patients simply accepted their lot as a voiceless victim-inmate, the Hornbostels stood up for themselves as well as the others, fighting the system when the time was right.

Hans accepted invitations to speaking engagements, fought to get the Louisiana legislature to give voting rights to the disenfranchised Carville patients, and railed against the rules under which his wife now lived, especially the loss of freedom.

"My wife lived in a Jap prison camp behind a barbed wire fence for three years," he said hotly. "And now she has a fence around her for a couple more years. There's no reason for that fence around the colony. These people aren't criminals. It's the most damnable thing I ever heard of. The state of Louisiana is treating these intelligent, good American people like so many criminals or insane."

He penned a bylined story, which ran in newspapers across the country, for the Associated Press, pointing out that "ignorance and prejudice cause infinitely more suffering than the disease itself." He pledged to dedicate the rest of his life to "trying to correct the wrong that is done lepers."

Indirectly, the unprecedented media attention generated by the Hornbostel case showed millions of Americans that leprosy was still an issue and that there was a place called Carville where human beings who happened to have a disease were being treated as prisoners.

32

INDEPENDENCE

Manila was still in rubble, and the stench of death still filled the nostrils of the living. Its residents still walked down bomb-blasted streets and stood on wrecked corners and told stories about stolen watches and stolen wives, about seeing guts on guava trees and the layers of burning tires and bodies. The victors counted 1,000 American dead, along with some 16,665 Japanese and more than 100,000 residents of Manila. By May 1946, Irene Murphy, head of the Private Philippine War Relief Mission, had tallied that 10,000 Filipinos had died of starvation since the war's end, mostly in the northern Luzon mountains. She predicted another 50,000 would die unless relief came.

War had refused to subside long after Gen. Douglas MacArthur had declared victory. So, too, had the debate about whether Mac-Arthur should have been so insistent on taking the Philippines at such a high human cost. "Those who had survived Japanese hate did not survive American love," wrote Carmen Guerrero, whose husband had been shot and who saw her aunt beheaded. "Both were equally deadly, the latter more so because [it was] sought and longed for."

But on July 4, 1946, the criticism was hard to find. Sirens screamed and church bells rang and Filipinos hustled down Dewey Boulevard. Dignitaries from fifty nations and more than two hundred thousand Filipinos gathered in their best clothes at the Queen

City's broad green Luneta, overlooking the bay, crowded with bobbing ships representing the world's commerce.

MacArthur would take the ship-shaped stage, in front of a statue of hero and revolutionary Jose Rizal, followed by Manuel Roxas, fifty-four, the first president of the first official Republic of the Philippines. The American flag would come down in a sweltering wave of emotion over the field not far from Intramuros, replaced by the Philippine national emblem, a sun with three stars. New soldiers would march in new boots.

Through rolling rain showers, the masses would witness the culmination of Manifest Destiny, the end of a disappointing forty-eight-year adventure in American colonialism seven thousand miles from the West Coast. Or at least the pretense of the end.

Magellan discovered the Philippines for Spain and the white man in 1521, and now, four hundred years later, after teaching missionary priests, after the gold, pearl, and hemp trade, after wars between the Spanish and the Dutch and the Spanish and the British, after revolution and assassination and American occupation, the Philippines were finally being granted independence, the first time in history an imperial nation relinquished a possession. American influence had left a little jazz, a love of fast cars, decent schools and American industry, and some impervious infrastructure. But gone were the docks and airfields and country clubs. Gone was the Manila Hotel and the sugar-cake houses of the wealthy. Gone was the national economy, the export trade, and half the carabao population, on which farmers staked their livelihoods. Next to Warsaw, Manila was the world's most destroyed city. Now the newest and poorest nation on earth needed help to survive its very first month.

Paul McNutt, the retiring US high commissioner and the first US ambassador to the Philippine Republic, read a statement from President Truman: "The United States of America hereby withdraws and surrenders all rights, possession, supervision, jurisdiction, and control of sovereignty now existing and exercised by the United States of America in and over the territory and people of the Philippines and on behalf of the United States I do hereby recognize the independence of the Philippines as a separate self-governing nation and acknowledge the authority and control over the same by the Government instituted by the people thereof under the Constitution now in force.

"A nation is born," he said. "Long live the Republic of the Philippines! May God bless and prosper the Filipino people and keep them safe and free."

MacArthur, greeted by a standing ovation as he took the stage, said, "Let history record this event in the sweep of democracy through the earth as foretelling the end of the mastery of peoples by the power of force alone—the end of empire as a political chain which binds the unwilling weak to the unyielding strong."

Roxas called American friendship "the greatest ornament of our independence."

"Any doubts which may still linger in some quarters of the earth as to the benign intentions of America should be resolved by what she so nobly and unselfishly accomplished here," he said. "Subtract the influence of the United States from the rest of the world and the answer is chaos."

The *Philippines Free Press* echoed the sentiments of the loyal and fiercely jealous islanders: "There are great days in the lives of all peoples—red-letter days, epoch-making days immortalized in verse and story and figured bronze and sculptured marble—days enshrined in the human heart and commemorated in joyous celebration or solemn observance," read the lead editorial. "Such a day has come to the Filipino people, bearing on its wings that idolized and cherished word—INDEPENDENCE."

33

SPOTLIGHT

The headline ran above the fold in the broadsheet *Manila Times* on January 18, 1947, a full eighteen months after Joey's letter found its way to Miss Marie Dachauer in Sacramento. The exposé was written by A. H. Lacson, a former Ateneo student and guerrilla scout.

ATROCIOUS CONDITIONS IN LEPER CAMP

Filth, misery, starvation, and inhuman conditions in general exist in the government leprosarium at Novaliches, Rizal, about 15 miles northeast of Manila, according to persons who joined a group headed by Miss Aurora Quezon that visited the place yesterday. Among those in the group were a United States Army chaplain and a nurse.

There are 650 lepers living in unspeakable conditions in that "graveyard of the living dead," according to one of the visitors, and this, he said, is due to official neglect and public indifference.

It was disclosed that there are only four nurses, three female and one male, attending to 650 lepers who are in dire need of medical attention. There not being enough beds, the majority of the patients sleep on the dirty floors. There is shortage of medicine as well as food, it was revealed.

The ration of one patient per week, it was pointed out, consists of a chupas of rice, 1 kilo of meat, 6 pieces of fish, and 3 tablespoons of sugar. The lepers have to cook their own food, usually in discarded tin cans. They have to walk a distance to get their rations, and when it rains, they slosh through mud.

The patients have to wash their own clothes and provide themselves with soap if they can. The toilets and other facilities are in lamentable state, completely unsanitary, according to the visitors.

As a result of malnutrition, it is said, six or seven patients die every month, although deaths from leprosy are low.

The story was followed the next day by another exposé in the same prominent position on the front page, headlined LEPERS ILL-FED, LACK MEDICINE, SURVEY SHOWS.

Food, clothes, bedding, and other articles that mean comfort to a normal individual are sadly undersupplied, the patients of this central Luzon leprosarium at Tala, Novaliches, Rizal, disclosed yesterday to a *Manila Times* representative.

And another followed on January 22: LEPERS' RICE RATIONS HIKED; CONDITIONS UNIMPROVED, CLAIM.

And another on January 26: HOPE FOR THE ALMOST HOPELESS.

Hope came to the almost hopeless inmates of the Central Luzon leprosarium in Tala, Novaliches when Miss Aurora Quezon and a group of social welfare workers dropped in recently and found the place filthy, and living conditions not conducive to the well-being of lepers.

A colony of only ten strong-material buildings with a normal capacity of 300, it is now housing over 600. There are only four nurses (three female and one male) to take care of all the inmates. There is a dearth of cots and most of the patients sleep on the floor.

Food, according to one patient, is meager; according to another, it is not fit for human beings. The diet is lacking in nutritious foods needed for repair of the worn-out tissues.

According to Dr. Marciano Carreon, chief of the leprosaria section of the bureau of health, a colony of 600 inmates should have at least 40 strong-material buildings. The overcrowding in that leprosarium has been partly eased with the construction of about 60 shacks in the neighborhood of the main colony. The government supplied most of the materials; the stronger-bodied lepers built the shacks. The only problem still remaining is the installation of water pipes to furnish the shack inhabitants with water so that they may be saved the strenuous task of securing their water supply from the main buildings.

Isolated as they are from the rest of the world, these lepers have not altogether lost faith in human kindness. There is one among them who has shown thoughtfulness for her fellow-sufferers and has consistently maintained the last frail link to faith in humanity, that they could not help holding on to it like drowning persons.

This "ministering angel" is Mrs. Joey Guerrero of Manila, who, finding life suddenly unkind to her, still clings to the idea that she is not entirely unwanted. There, with her, are people who need charity and she never lets a chance to alleviate their sufferings go past her. The children, in particular, look up to her; she has become more of a mother than a mere co-patient.

The stronger patients who do not require much attention lead practically a normal life. Some of them cultivate gardens from which they harvest vegetables to supplement their meager food rations. Others engage in pursuits quite in keeping with their ability.

The government finally sent investigators to the leprosarium, and they inspected the dormitories and medical facilities and eventually confirmed the press's findings. The *Times* story on January 29, 1947, was headlined ANOMALIES IN LEPER CAMP CONFIRMED: "The probers found that a patient, Mrs. Guerrero, really spends money out of her own funds for the washing of the children's clothes. She also provided lumber for the coffins of inmates who died in the station." The previous year, there had been thirty-six deaths, and the primary cause was beriberi.

Baby Quezon's clout and connections to those who succeeded her father in power at Malacañang Palace and to A. H. Lacson, who would go on to become mayor of Manila, had been key. But perhaps her lack of fear was most important. At a time when leprosy victims still carried a harsh stigma of being unclean, when it was still widely believed that the disease was spread through touch or simply inhaling the same air someone suffering exhaled, she maintained her friendship with her childhood classmate. Her own family would long remember Baby's stories about her work at Tala and her friend Joey. "She used to tell us stories about this friend who had leprosy," her sister, Zeneida "Nini" Quezon Avancena, would say much later. "Typical of my sister, she had no fear of being contaminated. She was more concerned about Joey thinking that she would be afraid of picking up the dread disease. So she had no hesitation in putting her arms around her and sharing food from her plate."

And once the cleansing spotlight of newspaper journalism shone upon a wretched corner of Philippine society, even the pencil pushers in the cold bureaucracy of the world's newest and poorest nation had empathy.

34

DISCOVERY

Ann Page's letter excited Joey. Resigned to death, the idea of life filled Joey's soul. The idea that the answer to five more years or ten more years or even a full recovery might be found in a forgotten little town on the banks of the Mississippi River kept her awake at night. She was also enthused to receive a visit from Dr. Leo Eloesser of San Francisco, a renowned thoracic surgeon and personal doctor and lifelong friend of the famed Mexican artist Frida Kahlo. Leo had worked among the neediest in rural postwar China under the auspices of the United Nations Relief and Rehabilitation Administration (UNRRA) and taught for the World Health Organization, and he was planning to return to teach lay volunteers about sanitation and communicable diseases, first aid and treatment of injuries, and midwifery. During Leo's stopover at Tala Leprosarium, he struck up what would become a lifelong friendship with Joey.

The two bonded over their love of music—Leo played viola with members of the San Francisco Symphony in an ensemble that met in his apartment each Wednesday—and their devotion to art and literature, but they also spoke of Carville and the medical breakthroughs there. After his visit, Joey wrote Leo to update him on the work of their mutual friend Frank Gaines, former mayor of Berkeley, California, who had helped set up the UNRRA offices in the Philippines after the war, and to ask if he'd given any more thought to trying to cure leprosy. She was again careful not to ask for too much, but was hoping for a miracle.

September 30, 1947

Dear Doctor Eloesser,

I have thought often of you, strange as that may seem, although you would not think that from my apparent indifference. Yet, I really have. Why, I don't know except perhaps the fact that you bothered to come and visit us, to eat and talk with me, a leper, and because your mind fascinated me. Being stupid, brilliant minds hold a magic fascination for me, although, it upsets me for it makes me realize how little I know, and how completely ignorant of many things which I am supposed to know. I know I enjoyed your visits and wished you could have stayed longer and visited with us longer. I would have wanted to get you interested in Hansen's disease with as much avidity as you have for tuberculosis—perhaps, you, in your great interest for the sufferings of others, might find the solution to the cure. Sometimes, I have asked, why not you? Mr. Gaines, being practical and in accord with your mind, tells me, that your love is for tuberculosis, and let someone else do the trick with Hansen's. Unfortunately, I am only a patient, or I would say, "But they tell me, it is practically the same in many ways—so why not Dr. Eloesser?" Well, when you have leisure time (or do you ever have it?), quien sabe? I dare say you want to know how things are with us?

Far better than when you were here. We have a permanent chaplain now, a Father Anthony L. Hofstee, O.P., who was formerly chaplain of the 13th Air Forces at McKinley. He has done wonders with things in general. We now have more social activities, as well as having started cooperative farming and poultry. The wards are cleaner and brighter, and the cottages are more orderly than they ever were. We needed such a one like him here, full of spirit and cheer, raring to go and do things. I have been very unwell, actually it is the reason for my failure to write to you sooner. I have had bouts and bouts of fever, my skin opening everywhere. It has left me pretty spent and very tired. For the past three weeks, I have had no fevers, my appetite is back to normal and I have only four wounds unhealed. I think I am safely out of the woods now. There is so much to do, so many things to accomplish and time is short. I wish I could get well.

I think you know of plans about Carville. However, that seems a long way off. We are waiting for General Parran's approval or papers which will be the sesame to open Carville's doors for me, the key lies in his hands. Leprosy being a mandatory quarantinable disease, they will not issue my passport and clearance here without a recommendation from the Surgeon-General. I am anxious to go to Carville—I feel that I might be able to achieve a cure there. God willing, if I can achieve a cure, it will mean so much for my fellow patients everywhere, for I can become a sort of symbol, a symbol for hope and greater courage. I believe in miracles and God will see that I am cured, if that is for my good, it will come.

It was a pleasure to have met you and made your acquaintance, and I hope that distance and time will not make you think of less of us here. I know I shall remember you always. You have my sincerest wishes for greater success.

Sincerely always,
Joey Guerrero

When Leo arrived in Tien Tsin, China, a few weeks later, he couldn't help but see what he could do for Joey. In December, he wrote to Dr. Herman Hilleboe, the state commissioner of health for New York, explaining Joey's story in detail, telling how her maps of the city helped US bombers "hit the Jap targets right tic tac toe," how she had sacrificed so much to help win the war.

"It seems that special permission of Surg. Gen. Parran is needed for her to pass the US mandatory quarantine and to gain admission," he wrote. "If governmental gratitude or recognition can cut governmental red tape then Guerrero deserves its being done, and I am writing to you to see whether I might enlist your efforts in her behalf."

In January 1948, Henderson forwarded Eloesser's letter to his friend Ralph Williams, assistant surgeon general at the US Bureau of Medical Services in Washington, DC. "If there is anything you can do for this friend, I am sure that it will be worthwhile," he wrote. "Doctor Eloesser is a wonderful man and I know that he would not ask for help if it was not needed."

But Williams had reservations. The United States had never before granted a visa to a foreigner with leprosy. Doing it now, for Joey, would be unprecedented.

"There are two points which I feel should be very carefully considered," he wrote. "The first is the possibility of difficulty in securing transportation by steamship or airplane for a person with leprosy. The second is that facilities exist in the Philippine Islands for the treatment of leprous persons with sulfones according to methods developed at Carville."

He suggested placing Joey in the care of a doctor in Manila, José Rodriguez, who had spent time at Carville and knew how to administer sulfones. "To bring Mrs. Guerrero from her friends and relatives in the Philippines to Carville, where the mode of life and entire surroundings would be completely different from that to which she has been accustomed all her life would probably not be satisfactory, as undoubtedly she would soon become homesick and lonely," Williams wrote. "It is, therefore, my well-considered suggestion that she secure sulfone treatment in the Philippines. If, for any reason, it is not practicable for her to be placed under the treatment of Dr. Rodriguez, I believe that the American Mission to Lepers or the Leonard Wood Memorial would take a special interest in this case to assure that a competent physician in the Philippines is furnished with the necessary sulfone drugs so that Mrs. Guerrero may be given proper treatment."

It was true that Dr. Rodriguez was a distinguished authority on Hansen's disease in the Philippines. He had visited the United States in 1946 on a fellowship from the Leonard Wood Memorial and on special detail from the Philippine Bureau of Health and was greeted by the Hornbostels when he arrived in Carville to study for a month. They thanked him for the part the Filipinos played in helping American prisoners of war. Rodriguez started his work with Hansen's disease twenty-five years before in Cebu but was transferred to Manila just before the outbreak of war. He opened an emergency hospital in Pampanga that gave aid to many sick Filipino and American soldiers during the death march, then helped secure food for starving patients on Culion. But even Rodriguez knew how hard it still was to get medicine in the islands. He'd been treating eight thousand patients before the war with the old chaulmoogra oil until food was cut off. Many of his patients starved to death. After the war, only twenty-five hundred were accounted for in the colonies, and no one knew how many remained in hiding. The previous March, Rodriguez himself reported that conditions in the Philippines' various leprosariums were "very difficult." Even though the government was still spending a third of its health budget on Hansen's disease, he said, the cost of everything had grown so high that the funds could barely be stretched beyond subsistence.

The best doctor with no access to medicine is not the best doctor. If they wanted to get Joey to Carville, if they wanted to get her healed, they'd need to appeal to a higher power.

35

RETURN TO THE ROCK

M aj. Gen. George Moore stood once again on Corregidor on October 12, 1947, the noon sun blazing above the parade grounds on Topside. The strains of "The Star-Spangled Banner" rolled out over the once doughty fortress at the mouth of Manila Bay as a few soldiers slowly lowered the American flag for the last time.

Moore looked on as a color guard of the US Army's Philippine scouts folded the flag with dignified snaps and presented it to Capt. Vincente Athambra of the Philippine Army. A Philippine color guard then hoisted the garrison flag of the Philippine Republic while the band played the Philippine anthem. Behind Moore, among the four hundred guests there for the ceremony, stood thirty survivors of the five-month siege and fall of Corregidor. They'd lost eight hundred fellow soldiers here and many more in the prisoner-of-war camps after surrender. Their discarded dog tags were buried in the island's dust.

When the Spanish claimed the island in 1793, it was used as an entry station for ships headed into Manila Bay, a place for the Spanish regulators to check and adjust shipping records. They called it Isla de Corregidor, *corregidor* literally meaning "corrector." This ceremony was something of a correction, an end to American imperialism. It also marked the acknowledgment of a new kind of warfare and the sudden obsolescence of an island once thought to be one of the most strategically important spots in the Pacific theater. More than $50 million went into building up Corregidor's tunnels and defenses, but, as eleven thousand American and Filipino survivors found out, advances in air power had made the Rock seem outmoded. The Philippines republic would use Malinta Tunnel for storage of small arms and ammunition. The rest of the grounds would house memorials to the soldiers of three nations who died defending this spit of land.

President Manuel Roxas addressed the crowd.

"We are deeply resolved that never again shall we be forced to let a harsh invader transgress upon our sacred land and home," he said. "We must keep our forces ready for all eventualities and for preservation of peace in the Pacific. This is an unshakable obligation for the republic as a signatory of the United Nations charter and as a completely sovereign democracy."

In accepting the transfer, Roxas said, "The American flag was lowered this time in victory, a victor of democracy, of justice, of love of freedom, and undying devotion to the cause of peace all over the world."

He recalled what General MacArthur had said long ago about the island: "Corregidor needs no comment from me. It has sounded its own story at the mouths of its guns."

Those guns were silent now, replaced by the surf lapping at the shoreline and grown men choking back tears.

Moore was emotional. He had spent much of his career right here.

"It was on this very spot that I suffered the most bitter experience of my life," he said. "Certainly I can say that my best years as a soldier have been spent on Corregidor. It would be difficult for me to portray my feelings or those of my troops on May 6, 1942, when I was directed by the overall commander to have my command lay down its arms at noon. We had fought a good fight and it was through no fault of our own that we were laying down our arms."

Moore said the transfer of the island to the Philippines carried with it "the warmest wishes of all Americans" and that "it is our sincere hope and firm belief that until the end of history no flag other than that of the republic of the Philippines shall ever fly over the hallowed ground of Corregidor."

36

ALL THAT IS CHANGED

Eleven months after the newspaper series about the scandalous conditions at Tala Leprosarium, a photographer from the *Philippines Free Press* drove over bumpy roads to the outskirts of Manila, to see if anything had changed. He found new dormitories and a new chapel. He heard a buzz saw cutting wood, and the sound of hammers on nails rang through the jackfruit and *duhat* trees. Some of the eighty children in residence were playing basketball barefoot on an open-air court. The hospital wards were clean and staffed by doctors in white coats. He found a stringed orchestra made up of leprosy victims, and before them he saw a little woman named Joey, a wisp over five feet tall, dancing with a patient.

He spent the rest of the day snapping photographs of a place once called "atrocious" and now greatly changed. His essay and photographs ran in the *Philippines Free Press*, November 22, 1947, between advertisements for new made-in-Holland Phillips radios and Omega watches, distinguished for beauty. TALA REVISITED, it was called.

> Early this year the shocking condition of the Tala (Central Luzon) Leprosarium was exposed to the horrified gaze of the public by Newspaperman A. H. Lacson. Lacson fittingly described the place as a "hell-hole." The gov-

ernment issued denials as usual, then explanations, then
mitigations, but the atrocious fact remained that the lepers, condemned by their disease to a life of suffering and
ostracism, had been further sentenced by official neglect
and indifference to greater suffering, to a life of hunger,
nakedness, and filth.

All that is changed. Suffering, natural to the disease,
remains, but now there is proper care for the unfortunate victims of the disease. Public opinion, stirred by the
press, compelled reform. The government listened to the
plaints of the lepers and moved. Something was done for
the forgotten ones. A miracle took place.

Today, patients in the dormitories are all sleeping on
beds and cots, none on the floor. Six hundred spring beds
from Surplus Property and 50 brand new hospital beds
from the UNRRA have been acquired in addition to old
beds and cots. The lepers sleep well—or as well as their
condition permits.

Water points have been extended, giving inmates living in cubos water facilities. Rations are distributed in a
shed where the patients need not walk far to get their
needs. All patients have been issued blankets and clothing, aside from relief received from other sources. The
food ration is served in variety, with ice cream once a
month.

For the construction of Quonset barracks and dormitories to prevent over-crowding and for repairs on
damaged buildings the sum of P160,000 has been appro-
priated. Four Quonsets have been erected so far and are
now occupied by inmates of the leprosarium. Telephone
service has even been installed within the compound for
emergency calls, etc.

"Dormitories are very much cleaner now than 10
months ago," the authorities point out—an admission

and an achievement. A stage has been constructed for the holding of programs and other entertainments. The lepers need a laugh.

Promin and diasone are now available to the inmates in limited quantities and research is going to improve the treatment of the disease. Nursing aids have been increased and two more nurses will be added to the present staff of three. A dentist and a laboratory technician and several relief workers have been added to the list of personnel while laboratory facilities and the operating room have been improved with the acquisition of more surgical instruments from the UNRRA and the Surplus Property Commission.

Toilets and other plumbing works have been repaired, ground improvement and beautification are in progress while mechanized farming will be introduced as soon as the tractor and farm implements are received from the UNRRA.

Conditions in the leprosarium today are indeed a far cry from what they were 10 months ago, and the authorities responsible for the change may congratulate themselves on a good job. For once the government has not stood in the way of improvement but has undertaken it.

Tala revisited shows what the government can do when, after prerequisite prodding by the press, it gives a damn. It is a feather in the cap of the government. Let us hope it will not be the only one.

37

MEDALS

Twenty miles outside of Manila, Joey put on her best dress and ran a comb through her black hair, parting it to the side. She stepped out of her little room filled with books and walked to the open-air chapel, where nearly a thousand ambulatory leprosy patients had gathered on May 29, 1948, a warm Saturday. Her friends congratulated her when she approached. She wasn't sure how any of this came to be, or which of her friends had written letters, but she humbly enjoyed the attention.

She took her place onstage between Gen. George Moore, defender of Corregidor, who was promoted from major general after the war, and Francis Cardinal Spellman, archbishop of New York, the man who had promised the Quezon family all those years ago at St. Patrick's Cathedral that he would not forget the valor of Filipinos.

Moore was holding it together. He had seen a lot during the war, especially after Corregidor, when he had bounced from prison camp to prison camp in Manila, Formosa, and then Manchuria. He once saw a Filipino woman carrying a baby. When she didn't bow low enough to a Japanese sentry, the sentry ran his sword through the infant, then through the screaming mother. Moore had been slapped and beaten and felt the rage rise up in his throat. He'd seen his comrades die. Retirement was coming, though, and days like this, when he got to honor the heroes of the war, were good.

When the crowd quieted, Moore began to read a citation. He held in his hand a Medal of Freedom with Silver Palm, President Truman's idea of how to honor foreign civilians who had resisted occupation and done something courageous to save American lives. Moore told the crowd that the work Mrs. Guerrero did in feeding internees and learning Japanese military secrets showed "more courage than that of a soldier on the field of battle." With that, he pinned the bronze medal, the second highest military decoration for a foreign civilian, to her dress amid cheers. Cardinal Spellman then called her a "heroine of the cross" for her work during the war and then at the leprosarium, and he pinned over her heart the Cardinal Spellman Medal, for "Christian fortitude and concern for fellow sufferers." She would cherish them both.

38

FRIENDS OF FRIENDS

Father Fred Zimmerman never met an outcast he didn't love. The balding Jesuit spent his life ministering to junkies in the slums, covering Mass in the black parishes, and shooting pool with ex-cons in smoky barrooms. And when he worked as a chaplain for the Pacific Air Service Command at Nichols Field in Manila just after the war, he took to driving two hours over bumpy roads every Sunday to visit the afflicted at Tala and especially his friend Joey. He never came empty handed and he never forgot about her even after his stint as chaplain ended and he wound up as head of Queen's Work in St. Louis, Missouri. They corresponded by mail, and when he learned of her predicament and learned that there was a slight possibility that she could get permission to travel to Carville for treatment, he sat down and fashioned a passionate letter to a friend of a friend, Eugene Cronk, vice president and treasurer of the D'Arcy Advertising Company in St. Louis, which represented Coca-Cola and had offices in Atlanta and New York. Zimmerman had learned from the newspaper that things were falling into place, but the consul general of Manila had refused to grant Joey a visa and referred the case instead to US attorney general Tom Clark.

"I worked with Joey Guerrero in the Philippines during the war and if there ever was a heroine, she was one," Zimmerman wrote on June 9, 1948. "No one knows how many American lives she saved by her underground work against the Japs and by her unbelievable exploits leading the first American troops into Manila. I think everything should be done to allow her a temporary visa in order to receive treatment at Carville. . . . Since the decision now rests with Attorney General Clark I am in hopes something can be done in getting him to give a favorable decision. According to arrangements her trip to the States in an Army plane is to start June 14th. I think Mr. McDonald's idea was to have you persuade Mr. Hannegan to put in a word for Joey with Attorney General Clark. Anything you can do will be appreciated."

Mr. Hannegan was Robert E. Hannegan, a St. Louis politician who had served the last three years as chairman of the Democratic National Committee and helped save Harry Truman's political career. He was now co-owner of the St. Louis Cardinals of Major League Baseball, and he was also very close with Attorney General Tom Clark, a Democrat, sending him ties, birthday greetings, and postcards from Ireland. Clark attended Hannegan's mother's funeral and enrolled Hannegan's family in the Bear Creek Orchards' Fruit-of-the-Month Club. So when Cronk forwarded Zimmerman's letter to Hannegan and Hannegan forwarded it to Clark, it carried enough weight to make it to the Justice Department desk of the attorney general himself.

> Dear Tom,
> I enclose a letter that was sent to Gene Cronk, a dear personal friend of mine, by Father Zimmerman, S.J. I do hope that you might be able to help Joey Guerrero. If so, let me know.
> Kindest regards and all good wishes.
>
> Sincerely,
> Bob

When the letter arrived, the US Public Health Service suddenly changed its position. Assistant Surgeon General Ralph Williams wrote again to Herman Hilleboe, Dr. Eloesser's friend and commissioner of health at the New York State Department of Health.

"Authorization has been given by the Public Health Service for the admission for treatment of Mrs. Joey Guerrero, the wife of a physician of Manila, Philippine Islands, to the National Leprosarium at Carville, Louisiana," Williams wrote. "Mrs. Guerrero rendered valuable service to the American Army during World War II. In recognition of this, the United States Government recently awarded her the Medal of Freedom. Her case has been given special consideration by the Public Health Service in response to numerous requests from many sources. In view of the recommendation of the physician in charge of the case in the Philippine Islands and because of the many unusual circumstances relative to this patient, the Public Health Service agreed to accept her as a special study case if she presented herself at Carville. . . . Upon her arrival at Carville, a careful study will be made of her case to determine the type of treatment best fitted to her individual needs."

On June 14, newspapers across the country carried a brief with the news.

"She is or will soon be on her way," Clark wrote back to Hannegan. "It was good to hear from you. We saw Bobby the other night at Mimi's dance. Give our best to Irma."

REGULATIONS WAIVED

MANILA—The US Consulate today received permission from Washington to waive regulations barring lepers and issue a visa for Mrs. Josefina Guerrero to go to Carville, La., for leprosy treatment. Mrs. Guerrero, a Filipino war heroine whose espionage was credited with saving many American lives, missed the American ship *Hope* in Manila Sunday because she lacked a visa.

39

CARVILLE

The patients, thirty or forty of them, woke before sunrise and gathered in their pajamas in front of the old plantation, under the live oaks dripping Spanish moss on the morning of July 11, 1948. They were joined by several of the Daughters of Charity of St. Vincent de Paul, the butterfly nuns, plainly dressed in their gray habits and tall white cornettes. The newsmen showed up, too, one from the Associated Press and one from the *Times-Picayune* in New Orleans. They stood in the moonlight, smoking cigarettes and chatting and waiting, as the bullfrogs croaked on the banks of the Mississippi River across the two-lane highway.

Carville's newest guest was due any minute. They didn't want to miss it.

When the inky black began to give way to the blue-gray haze of morning, they saw headlights swing around a bend. She was finally here.

Inside the car, Josefina Guerrero took a few deep breaths. She was still clutching an air-sickness bag and trying to hold down the nausea from her flight.

The driver spoke up.

"Here we are, Joey," he said. "This is Carville."

At last. She was thirty years old and she had woken up that morning with the same wish she had been making for years: Let this be the day when I will be cured, when the disease that lives inside me will be arrested so I can enjoy a real life. Six years before, her diagnosis had been a death sentence and, because of who she was and what she believed, that afforded her the opportunity to do great things. Now that she had tasted the possibility of a cure, the desire to live consumed her.

She had to come halfway around the world and cut through thickets of red tape, but now she was closer than ever.

Her journey was long. She'd come by ship, the USAT *General John Pope*, from Manila to San Francisco, where she was welcomed by more than three hundred soldiers, men whose lives she had saved and men she had nursed to health after the Battle of Manila. They cheered when she stepped off the gangplank, flashbulbs bursting, television cameras rolling, and reporters scribbling in their notebooks. Though the San Francisco doctor who examined her after the landing called her disease "advanced," the soldiers hugged her neck and stuck bouquets of roses in her arms and kissed her cheeks. They remembered her on the battlefield and outside the walls of Santo Tomas and walking through the cross fire. The courage she had shown during the war won her the adoration of brave men. A band played the Philippine national anthem. Her friend Frank Gaines was with her, along with the Philippine government consul general and Father Clement Barberich, who had paid Joey's passage. Citizens in the crowd waved their handkerchiefs as she stood there smiling, arms loaded with giant bouquets of flowers.

The scene was too much for the young woman with curly black hair who wore her Medal of Freedom pinned to her blouse. She stood just five feet tall and weighed one hundred pounds, but she seemed larger than life.

"This is more than I expected," she told the press.

The reporters didn't miss the significance of this defining moment. A newspaperman named John Chestnutt wrote in the *San Francisco Call-Bulletin*, "In other places and other, less enlightened times, there would have been no such welcome. Instead of being greeted she would have been, quite wrongly, shunned because of her illness."

After the celebration, she caught an air force plane to New Orleans, falling ill from nausea, and then ducked into an ambulance for the seventy-five-mile trip to Carville. She rolled down the window and felt the cool rush of wind against her face as they sped past rows of tidy houses and palmettos and zinnias on well-kept lawns. She saw the lights of downtown New Orleans and the black expanse of the mighty Mississippi and the cypress swamps thick with life.

"This is America," she thought.

She felt like she was finally waking from a bad dream and standing on the threshold of a new life as rural Louisiana blurred by outside the window.

When the ambulance came down the gravel two-lane road and stopped in front of the clinic at Carville and the door swung open, the patients began to cheer. One of the Filipino patients forced a sheaf of ferns and red roses into her arms as a flashbulb popped in the morning light. The photograph captured a woman wearing red lipstick on a giant smile, stepping out of an old ambulance with Marine Hospital stenciled on the rear doors. The Hornbostels, Gertrude and Hans, hugged her neck and praised her for her heroics.

"Welcome, Joey," said Stanley Stein, a blind man who was the editor of the patient newspaper. "Welcome to Carville."

She looked fresh and trim in a gray pencil-striped suit, white blouse, and summer costume jewelry. Someone remarked that she looked more like she was arriving at a fancy resort than a leprosy hospital. Joey was smiling but nervous.

"Thank you so much for the flowers," she said.

One of the nuns took her arm and led her down a long porch and then a quiet corridor to a temporary room with "13" painted on the door. Joey giggled when she saw it.

At the window was a runner of red, yellow, and blue wool made by another patient, and on it were woven the words Welcome Joey.

The room was filled with flowers. On a tray beside the bed sat a breakfast of grapefruit, warm toast, and drip coffee. Joey couldn't stop smiling.

Gertrude Hornbostel wanted to figure out the puzzle of how Joey had made it through enemy lines. Despite being at the center of attention during the race to Manila, the internees at Santo Tomas knew only what they heard through the grapevine and from their own intelligence gatherers. Hornbostel remembered hearing that when US troops got close to Manila, the Japanese planned to line the internees up in the courtyard and mow them down by machine-gun fire. She remembered hearing that a Nisei spy in the camp had found such orders on the desk of the Japanese commandant, notified the internee intelligence committee, then left camp to tell the guerrillas, with hopes they could inform MacArthur and tell him to hurry.

"Joey's exploits saved the lives of all those men who were rushing to save us by a 36-hour forced march," Hornbostel would write. "They raced with the other outfit to see which could get in first. But the biggest thing in our lives was the fact that they were there and that they were there in time—thanks to Joey, but at that time we did not realize that we owed our lives to this one little Filipino girl, although we had heard by grapevine about her mission. We did not know then that she had come through safely. All this knowledge had to be put together piecemeal from what little information we could glean here and there. It was like working out a crossword puzzle with the word that gave you the key to the whole list as 'Billy Ferrer,' Joey's name with the underground."

When she finished visiting with the doting Gertrude Hornbostel, Joey took a shower and changed clothes, and the nurse guided her into a spring bed with clean sheets—both rare luxuries back at Novaliches—and fluffed the pillows around her. Joey then opened the door for the newspapermen who had been waiting. She answered all their questions the best she could. About the trip. About how she was treated during her travels. About Tala.

"The Filipinos look upon leprosy as a curse," she said. "When I first got to the colony, conditions were vile. Patients were sleeping on the floor, living promiscuously, and the government could do nothing about it. So I took some patients and said, 'Let's see what we can do with a little lye and soap.' Before long we had it all cleaned up. Then I wrote my friends in California and the letter was published and we began receiving gifts of food and clothing from America. And the GIs, how they helped us! They would come and bring something, maybe only a candy bar, but something.

"In changing squalid and almost unspeakable conditions there to at least bearable, and in exposing such conditions, some of my friends and especially Aurora 'Baby' Quezon, daughter of our late President Quezon, stood valiantly by me," she said. The reporters "were fearless in their reporting. But I know I shall be able to serve the patients at Tala much better when I am well, and I fully expect to get well here now that I can receive treatment with the new sulfone drugs."

The Associated Press dispatch would run in papers across the country under the headline HEROINE AT LEPROSARIUM.

Mrs. Josefina Guerrero, who was known as Joey to the countless G.I.s she helped fight the Japanese in her native Philippines, arrived at the Carville National Leprosarium here today. She is the first foreigner ever to be accepted as a patient.

Mrs. Guerrero's journey to Carville had a dramatic touch early today. The plane carrying her from San Francisco hovered for 45 minutes over Harding Field at Baton Rouge, unable to land because of fog. It flew finally to New Orleans where a Carville ambulance met the heroine and brought her to the hospital here.

Mrs. Guerrero was permitted to enter the United States only after a special ruling from Attorney General Tom Clark. She was earlier unable to get a visa to leave

Manila because the United States immigration laws ban
the entry of lepers into this country.

"Being at Carville is like a homecoming," she told one reporter.
"I feel that we all met before because of our long correspondence."

To another she introduced a Chinese doll she was carrying. "I
have had her since I was in high school and look at her, how worn
she is getting," she said as she picked at her breakfast. "Her name is
Ah Choo—you know, like a little sneeze." She placed Ah Choo on
the pillow beside her as a nurse bustled about the room.

She told them the hardest thing about leaving was saying good-
bye to the children at Tala. She had bonded closely with many of
them, coming to think of them as her own.

"That's what I hated most," she said. "When I said good-bye,
they cried as though they were attending my funeral."

When the reporters left, she inspected her surroundings. There
was a ceiling fan and wall fan, a washbasin with hot and cold taps,
a rocking chair, a dresser with a mirror, window blinds to shut out
the sun. Three hundred letters addressed to her were stacked neatly
on a table. One young man brought in a huge confectioner's box.
Inside was a pink-and-white frosted cake rimmed with thirty tiny
candles and bearing the greeting: HAPPY BIRTHDAY. Stanley Stein
asked Joey if it was her birthday. "No," Joey laughed. "But it will be
soon. On August 5, and then I'll be very old, 31 years."

Joey was amazed. What comfort and luxury! But a sense of
sadness crept in when she remembered Novaliches and her friends
back home. If only there was a place like Carville in Manila. She fell
asleep with those thoughts. When she woke a few hours later, one
of the sisters told her she had several phone calls to return. Joey
was escorted down a long covered walkway, past rows of bicycles,
to the canteen, where a hushed quiet fell over the crowd when she
walked in.

"This is Joey," said the man escorting her.

"Hello, Joey," one of the patients said.

"Welcome, Joey," said another.

This was followed by a chorus of greetings from the patients. The ice was broken. Suddenly everyone was trying to help her.

"It's hot in here, isn't it?" someone asked. "Would you like a cold drink?"

"Dr. Pepper? 7-Up? Root beer?" someone else said.

"Ice cream, maybe?" said another.

In less than a minute, she had two dozen new friends.

Joey's escort showed her to the telephone booth, where she returned calls to even more reporters, patiently answering their questions. She was quickly becoming a darling of the news media. A radio show host from WWL New Orleans wanted to broadcast an interview with Joey from Carville. A photographer from the *New York Times* wanted to take a picture of her. A *Time* magazine correspondent wanted an interview for a story on the fight to bring her to the United States.

40

OLD FEARS

Not long before Joey arrived at Carville, many Americans wanted nothing to do with victims of leprosy. The hospital at Carville itself was the product of a fearful, uninformed public trying to deal with a "leper problem," as reporters called it.

"Leprosy is dreaded most of all diseases, not because it kills, but because it leaves alive; not for its pain—though painful at times, the loss of pain and tactile sensation is dreaded more," wrote Dr. Ernest Muir, a medical missionary among Bengal leprosy victims. "Mask face, unclosing eyes, slavering mouth, claw-hands and limping feet; or even worse, beetling brows, stuffed nose, ulcerating legs, and painful eyes drawing on towards blindness."

Americans thought of leprosy as a disease that happened elsewhere, in another country, another time. It was a nightmarish relic, and the afflicted seemed almost inhuman. So, in cases in which Americans contracted leprosy, the general sentiment was to ostracize the victim.

The case of John Ruskin Early, an American patriot, serves as a shining example of this national attitude. Early hailed from the Appalachian Mountains of North Carolina, and he served as a private in the Fifth United States Infantry during the Spanish-American War. He saw action in Cuba, where he contracted what he thought was malaria, before being sent with his unit to the Philippines. He quit the army to marry a girl, went to work back home in a pulp mill, and soon fell ill from the chemicals to which he was exposed. In August 1908, no longer well enough to work, Early decided to travel to Washington, DC, to seek his claim for a war pension. But his condition puzzled the medical authorities in the nation's capital. Soon they claimed to have discovered the leprosy bacteria in a skin sample they'd removed from his red and puffy face. He was immediately quarantined to a tent in a marshy spot on the Potomac River, where he awaited his fate.

No one knew what to do with Early. To send him back home to North Carolina violated the Contagious Diseases Acts of 1890 and 1893. Early's wife campaigned for his release, writing to President Taft and eminent leprologists, including the Norwegian physician Gerhard Armauer Hansen, who first discovered *Mycobacterium leprae*, the intracellular bacterium that causes leprosy. Mrs. Early's vigorous effort came to the attention of a New York City dermatologist who traveled to Washington to visit Early in 1909. The New York City Health Department didn't regard leprosy as so contagious as to require segregation, so the dermatologist arranged to treat Early in New York. Early was bundled into a boxcar with a Salvation Army medic who was instructed to destroy all eating and drinking utensils Early touched and to make sure the patient wore rubber gloves at all times. Once in New York, doctors could find no trace of the leprosy bacillus in Early's skin samples. He was soon cleared to leave on his own.

Early moved with his family to Virginia and found work on a farm, but when he returned to Washington to collect his pension, he was arrested and quarantined to the same tent he had lived in before. A spate of legal action followed, and he was again sealed in a boxcar and returned to New York. More troubling than his disease was his notoriety. The newspapers were up in arms.

Early and his family had nowhere to settle openly, so they fled to the West Coast and tried to make a home in Tacoma, Washington, but their secret was soon out, and the locals threw fits about

their new neighbors. The US surgeon general quarantined Early to
Port Townsend, Washington, where he stayed less than a year before
going on the lam. Early had hatched a plan to protest his mistreat-
ment. He secretly traveled back to the East Coast via Canada and,
using the alias E. J. Watson, checked into one of Washington's posh-
est hotels, the Willard, where several senators and representatives
and diplomats were staying. When the city's chief medical inspector
learned where Early was staying, he sprinted over and found Early
talking to a gaggle of newspaper reporters.

"I knew that if I mingled among the well-to-do and the rich and
exposed them to contagion," he told them, "that they would arise
out of self-protection and further my plan for a national home."

He was right. Congress went into a tizzy. One congressman said
Early wandering freely about the country was "worse than turning
loose a band of murderers." Another proposed banishing Early and
other victims to an Alaskan island. Early's plan had worked, and a
national leprosarium was suddenly part of the political agenda, but
it would be situated far from remote Alaska.

In 1909, when John Early was headed for isolation at Carville, a
survey of leprosy in the United States found 139 cases in fourteen
states. Fifty of them were in Louisiana, more than double the number from any other state.

Leprosy was first identified in Louisiana in the 1760s, and it was
believed the disease arrived during the slave trade or was brought
south by the French-speaking Acadians whom the British ousted
from Nova Scotia in the second half of the eighteenth century. Those
labeled lepers were mostly exiled to designated colonies or settle-
ments, the largest of which was located in lower Bayou Lafourche,
in the swamplands southwest of New Orleans. They lived a miserable existence amid the mosquitoes and alligators of the blackwa-
ter swamps. And sometimes they migrated to the cities. In the late
1800s, a considerable number had moved to New Orleans and were
mixing freely with the uninfected population. This was a source of
robust consternation for those not afflicted.

Like everywhere else, the New Orleans medical community held conflicting views of leprosy. It was infectious and contagious. It was hereditary and incurable.

In the 1890s, a New Orleans dermatologist named Isadore Dyer began trying to bring leprosy into the framework of science and medicine.

"Leprosy has always stood as the example of the most fearful of human afflictions," he wrote. "The Biblical estimate of the disease has created a popular horror which even down to modern times has placed the leper as a pariah and a person condemned by his state to abandonment. It must be classed among the contagious diseases, not as contagious as tuberculosis or syphilis, but still a menace of no mean importance, when it is considered that its spread is as constant as it is insidious and that its evidences are more horrible than most known diseases."

Dyer favored segregation as much for the protection of the healthy from the leprosy victims as to protect the "lepers" from the healthy. He was critical of the keeper of a "pest house" for leprosy patients in New Orleans. A muckraking young journalist from the *Daily Picayune* wrote a series of articles in the 1890s exposing the horrible conditions at the place, much like A. H. Lacson would later do with Tala. The series and Dyer's preaching finally convinced the state legislature of the need to form a State Board of Control for the Leper Home in order to find a permanent site for a new colony where patients could live.

The idea was to isolate those afflicted and also provide treatment and nursing by those willing. But no sooner was a site selected, no matter how remote, than protest raged against it. The commission thought it had secured a fine site on the shores of Lake Pontchartrain, twenty miles from the nearest house. But as soon as it was announced, those who lived around the lake raised holy hell. They complained that waste runoff and hospital debris would wash up on their shores and spread the disease. The "leper commission" buckled under the pressure and started its search anew.

The commission soon set its sights on an abandoned slavery-era
sugar plantation on the Mississippi River called Indian Camp, in
Iberville Parish, not far from a prosperous town called White Castle.
The ruse to the locals was that the 337-acre plantation was being
converted into an ostrich farm, and the commission quietly transformed the dilapidated antebellum mansion into a hospital and the
slave quarters into dormitories for the new patients. The plantation
had room for one hundred lepers.

After dark on November 31, 1894, seven of the ten inmates
at the pest house were loaded onto carts and driven to the New
Orleans wharf in secrecy, where Dyer and a few journalists were
waiting. The group climbed aboard a coal barge, and a tug started
churning north on the black Mississippi toward Indian Camp.

They couldn't keep the plan quiet for even twenty-four hours.
As soon as the sun came up, the ten-year-old son of the local post-
master rode his pony to the top of the levee to catch sight of the
ostriches that were supposed to be coming.

"Lordy, Lordy, little boss," said his companion, an elderly black
man. "Them's no ostriches—them's sick folks!"

When locals finally figured out what was going on, they protested vigorously, signing a petition and threatening violence. But it
was too late. The Louisiana Leper Home opened in 1894, the first
leprosarium in the United States.

But difficulties remained. First, the locals didn't want them
there. They refused to sell bread and supplies to the hospital, so
goods had to be shipped upriver from New Orleans. The servants
and nurses at the hospital were warned they'd be shot if they set
foot off the grounds. Besides that, the patients didn't like the idea
of being confined or in some cases forced to leave behind their husbands or wives or children. Some simply refused to go. State officials decided that the inert and stubborn victims would be rounded
up, but no law enforcement officers were happy about orders to
hunt down lepers, physically round them up, and transport them to
Carville. The last time the Board of Health had sent a commission

down Bayou Lafourche to examine the lepers in the largest colony in the state, the afflicted were scared they were going to be captured and imprisoned, so they fled deep into the swamps to hide.

Little by little during the following decades, improvements were made at the hospital, and patients began to migrate voluntarily. And they began to make Carville home. They grew vegetable gardens and decorated their rooms and argued for modern conveniences like hot plates and bicycles. Some of them married and built their own homes on the hospital grounds from scrap materials and salvaged wood. The patients organized and convinced hospital authorities to improve the facilities. They got a soda fountain, a swimming pool, a telephone booth, and a modern lounge.

Most of the amenities were a direct result of the work of patient no. 746, Stanley Stein.

41

CRUSADER

Stanley Stein arrived at Carville in 1931, seventeen years before Joey, carrying copies of the *New Yorker* and *Theater Arts* and dressed in a Brooks Brothers topcoat, a natty tweed suit, a perfectly knotted foulard, and spats. Rumor spread among the patients that he was a millionaire from New York.

The truth was, Stein was a Texan, born and raised outside San Antonio, with a degree in pharmacology from the University of Texas. He had opened a drugstore in San Antonio after college, but his real love was the community's little Jewish theater. He wanted to be an actor and was chasing that dream when the first symptoms of leprosy started appearing on his skin.

In a century of rapid scientific advancement, the disease still carried a stigma, reinforced by confused biblical injunctions and historical medical ignorance. A doctor sent Stein to New York for treatment, but that doctor reported him as a leper, and almost overnight he was swept up and sent secretly by train to New Orleans, then to Carville. American quarantine laws required that leprosy victims be locked away without means to legally protest.

Stein's arrival was a culture shock. He noticed rows of barbed wire atop the tall cyclone fence surrounding the hospital, at the time called US Marine Hospital No. 66. He realized he was no longer free. He was in exile in his own country.

"Have you decided on your new name, young man?" one of the sisters asked him. Sidney Levyson was his birth name, but on arrival at Carville, he was encouraged to change it.

"Suddenly it all made sense," Stein would later write. "I was not just a sick man entering a hospital. I was a lost soul consigned to limbo, an outcast, and I must spare my family from any share in my disgrace. My mother, who adored me, had hidden my secret from her closest relatives. Uncle Berthold had almost fainted when he learned the truth. I myself had not wanted my friends and relatives to know what was wrong with me."

Stein was young, thirty-one, and educated, but this was new.

"You have done nothing to be ashamed of," the sister told him, "but there are some stupid people in the world and you must protect your loved ones from their stupidity. Perfectly healthy children have been denied the right to attend school because some member of their family was at Carville. Some patients have preferred that their friends believe them to be dead to save their families from abuse and ostracism. Choose a name you will be proud of someday."

Stanley Stein was born. With the change, his life suddenly seemed uncomplicated. He was soon studying leprosy, and the head nurse at Carville was happy to turn over her copies of the *International Journal of Leprosy* and *Modern Methods with an Ancient Scourge* for his research. Stein was surprised to learn his malady and the malady of the others at Carville had nothing whatsoever in common with the symptoms of the biblical "leprosy" in Leviticus 13: "When a man shall have in the skin of his flesh a rising, a scab, or bright spot, and it be in the skin of his flesh like the plague of leprosy; then he shall be brought unto Aaron the priest, or unto one of his sons the priests. And the priest shall look on the plague in the skin of the flesh: and when the hair in the plague is turned white, and the plague in sight be deeper than the skin of his flesh, it is a plague of leprosy: and the priest shall look on him, and pronounce him unclean."

Stein noticed off the bat that there was a sort of hopeless apathy hovering over the place. The listlessness with which his fellow inmates went about their daily lives sickened him. He couldn't understand why the laughter at Carville—what laughter there was—was of despair. He understood that they were all suffering from a disease that made half the world panic and flee, but it was less terrible than cancer and less contagious than syphilis.

He aimed to make the most of his new life as an outcast. He took a job, got a role in a patient play, and met new friends. Soon he convinced a few of them to help him start a patient newspaper, the *Star*, and gave it the motto: "Radiating the light of truth on Hansen's disease." The first issue was printed on May 16, 1931, two and a half months after Stein arrived, and it carried a sports column, social calendar, drama criticism, and a feature story about a hen caring for four baby kittens on the Carville campus. But a few short years later, the *Star* had become a trumpet for the rights of Carville patients and Hansen's victims all over. People took to calling Stanley Stein the Carville Crusader.

"It has long been recognized that 'It pays to Advertise.' We are convinced that it also pays to protest," he wrote in the *Star*. "Guided by our favorite axiom, 'to permit an error to go unchallenged is to participate in it,' THE STAR attacks any and all false statements about leprosy appearing in the press or magazines whenever they are brought to our attention, and with uncanny inevitability we hear about such statements. Sometimes our letters of protest are ignored, sometimes we get a polite brush-off, but in most cases the offending parties, after learning the truth, are willing to correct the error which they unwittingly expressed."

His early target was the word *leper*. Stein wanted to banish the word from the English language, and it was a frequent subject of editorials in the *Star*. He also took on the Catholic Church, which had an ancient custom of holding a "leper Mass" in which an afflicted person took part in his own funeral before being banished from his community.

To our minds, this ceremony is about the cruelest of practices that could ever be perpetrated in the name of religion. We can only contrast such a treatment with that of the Divine Savior, who healed the ten sufferers and left no instructions that they ever be treated in any other manner. We feel that the Church, both ancient and modern, has done more to keep the stigma of leprosy alive in the public mind than any other force. We admit, however, that they have done lots of good. Foreign missionaries are doing wonderful work among the half-civilized and starving victims of leprosy in other lands, ministering in a noble and heroic way to their needs, both spiritual and physical. But on the other hand, they are still influenced by the superstitions of the Dark Ages as related to our social status. We are still outcasts in their minds, and they still continue to hold the Leper Mass over us, though in a somewhat modified form. For the unfortunate victim, it is tragic indeed that leprosy, of the many loathsome diseases, should get mention in the Bible as a special sign of the Almighty's disfavor.

The blunt criticism offended some, but Stein was able to deftly navigate the system in which he was stuck and remain friendly with those he attacked in print. The chaplain at Carville, who had taken offense to the editorial about the "leper Mass," still supported Stein's very basic point that equating leprosy with sin was incorrect and discriminatory. Writing to publications that circulated among priests, such as the *American Ecclesiastical Review*, Father Abbot Paul warned his fellow pastors about unfairly linking the disease with sin.

Some preachers are apt to stress in detail the supposed horrors of the disease. In an effort to castigate prevailing vices, they may be tempted to draw a parallel between sin and sickness, in connection with leprosy. But, unlike some other diseases, leprosy is not caused by indecent and unclean living. In our hospital we have saints as well as sinners and they were saints before they contracted the disease.

One of Stein's most useful characteristics was his tenacious letter writing. He fired off hundreds—maybe thousands—of responses to newspaper and magazine editors and television and radio station managers who had printed or broadcast dusty, damaging myths about leprosy, or used the loaded word *leper* as a pejorative. He also often wrote to corporations using the word in advertising campaigns. He published in the *Star* an open letter to the makers of Absorbine Junior, which had launched a national advertising campaign that had as its slogan: "Don't be a locker-room leper!" Speaking for the citizens of Carville, he wrote, "We do not spread obnoxious infections such as those afflicted with athlete's foot may do."

Stein's letters were often stern but inviting. Learn about the disease, he'd write, so you can help us educate the public. Come visit Carville, he'd write, so you can erase the stigma. He had science on his side. Studies were showing that leprosy was not nearly as contagious as previously thought. Research showed that 95 percent of the US population was naturally immune to the disease. No doctor or nurse or nun or visitor to Carville had ever caught leprosy from a patient.

But even through the late 1940s, Stein consistently heard stories of Hansen's victims being stigmatized and ostracized. A few weeks before Joey's arrival, a Christian minister and head of a church on the West Coast showed up at the hospital with an incredible story of being run out of town.

Rev. C. E. Olmstead had a biopsy on a suspicious lesion on his right ankle. His dermatologist told him he had Hansen's disease. Worse, the doctor said he had informed the Los Angeles Board of Public Health, which gave Olmstead less than twenty-four hours to be out of his home and on his way to Carville for treatment. If he was found at home after noon the following day, he was told, he would be arrested and would be confined to L.A. County Hospital for six to eight months without treatment until they could get him approved for travel to Carville. Floored, the reverend sought urgent care for his elderly and blind mother, packed as quickly as possible, and left with his wife for Carville. On arrival, he learned that Los Angeles public health officials had quarantined his house and posted placards outside saying it was a dangerous place to enter. The minister was irate, but there was little he could do.

Stein gave him two columns in the *Star* to vent his frustrations.

"In a day of understanding, when they know Hansen's disease is far less infectious than tuberculosis which is never quarantined, I cannot see any but political considerations for the treatment I was given," Olmstead wrote. "Had I been given a week to settle my personal and church affairs, and get mother taken care of, I could now live here with a free mind. The community in which I lived, as well as the church in which I served as a minister could have been adequately informed so there would have been no paralysis or fear or suspicion. As it is, both are scared. One person tells another, the story gets more terrible with every telling. I am ruined in the community, except for those who know me well enough to believe that in spite of everything they can see, the quick departure and quarantine, there is still another side to the story, that one who has always been honorable could not be such a public menace as I have been labeled."

Stein's diligence earned him friends in the mainstream press, and they often took him up on his invitation to visit the hospital. Humanizing leprosy victims would go a long way toward edging greater America toward empathy. Then maybe, just maybe, patients like Reverend Olmstead—even Stanley Stein himself—wouldn't have to live out their lives confined behind rolls of barbed wire like prisoners. The only way Stein would see freedom was if he won the war against ignorance.

And that's where Joey came in. A humble heroine of one war already. A spy who saved hundreds, maybe thousands, of lives. A beautiful, nonthreatening young woman who loved watching ballet, writing poetry, and listening to classical music. And she just happened to have Hansen's disease. Stein refused to call it leprosy. The power of her story was no secret to those who understood the plight of the patients at Carville.

"I believe if anything significant is ever to be done for Lepers, it will have to be during the lifetime of Joey," wrote a man named George Doody, from Minnesota, who spent four years in a tuberculosis hospital and started a fund drive after reading Joey's story. "For if there was ever a story that would capture the imagination of the people of world, it would be the life of the Leper Heroine at Carville."

Stein saw her as their token, their spokesperson, a symbol to the world at large that Hansen's disease victims were humans, good and decent people. More than three hundred patients who, like Stein, had been captured and misunderstood and locked away behind fences and out of the conscience of Americans were now hopeful that Joey could bridge the divide, could make people understand.

They'd already adopted an anthem that represented this attitude: the Cole Porter song "Don't Fence Me In."

Stanley Stein had first heard of Joey three years before, in 1945, when Father Luis Torralba wrote of her plight to Marie Dachauer and Dachauer sent the letter to Father Abbot Paul at Carville. The chaplain turned the letter over to Stein, and he published it in the *Star*. Stein and other patients and citizens waged war on Joey's behalf, writing to officials who would eventually grant her permission to enter the United States, to come to Carville.

Now here she was, a woman rejected by her own community, commanding the spotlight. The patients were happy to see her. Hundreds of thousands of Americans were following her story in the newspapers. And Stanley Stein was plotting his next move to bring a better understanding of leprosy to the world.

As soon as she answered all her letters and returned all her phone calls, Stein inducted Joey into the *Star* staff. She was a fine typist, and she wrote excellent, lucid English. She seemed delighted to belong to the team that was putting out the newsletter she'd been reading at Novaliches for several years. While the circulation was fewer than ten thousand copies a month, Stein was mailing them to people all over the world, to leper colonies, hospitals, libraries.

What pleased him most was that Joey arrived carrying a typewriter.

42

FALLEN

BURLINGAME, Cal., December 4, 1949 (AP)—Major General George F. Moore, commander of Corregidor Fortress in the long Japanese siege, was found dead near a lonely mountain road last night, a bullet through his head and his service pistol in his hand.

The 62-year-old Texan and his wife, Lucille, had lived here since his retirement last August, after 40 years in the Army. Police Patrolman George Kurrell, who found the body, said a note was found near the general's hand. The note was addressed to General Moore's wife.

43

CONTROVERSY

A thousand years of misunderstanding is a formidable opponent, but Stanley Stein and his staff at the *Star* were up for the challenge. The man who had by then lost most of his eyesight to leprosy needed a massive Madison Avenue–style campaign to root out the misconceptions about leprosy. He staged his attack on several fronts. First, now that he had Joey and the Hornbostels and the celebrity they brought into Carville, he could leverage that goodwill for better media attention. And sure enough, on July 19, 1948, shortly after Joey's arrival, a story in *Time* magazine introduced Americans to Carville.

> When the Americans landed on Leyte, Joey gallantly took advantage of the Japs' dread of lepers to carry out her spying. Under the Japs' noses, she mapped the fortifications along the waterfront and the location of aircraft batteries along Dewey Boulevard. If she was stopped, she just pointed to her blotched face. Using her drawings, US planes from Mindoro blasted the batteries to smithereens. Her disease made her almost indifferent to her personal safety. When the guerrillas discovered a freshly sown minefield in the area where the 37th Division was scheduled to attack Manila, they picked Joey to get the

information through. They taped the map to her back, told her to make her last confession, and sent her off. For 56 miles Joey trudged through Jap encampments and check points. Several times she was stopped, dismissed after a perfunctory search. She delivered the map safely.

The piece generated more than four thousand letters to the editor of *Time*. Joey's celebrity, under the circumstances, was unprecedented. An editorial in the *Fort Worth Star Telegram* praised Attorney General Tom Clark for waving the immigration laws to let Joey into the Carville hospital and proved itself to be among progressive newspapers by concluding: "Mrs. Guerrero will be doing the nation—and mankind—another service if her cause helps to dispel some popular misconceptions about leprosy that have hampered proper treatment of the disease and have caused those afflicted with it to be subjected to unnecessary suffering." Following that, a crew from a national CBS radio and television broadcast called *We, the People* arrived and recorded interviews with Joey, the Hornbostels, Stanley Stein, and Dr. Frederick Andrew Johansen, also known as Dr. Jo, the longtime medical director at the leprosarium.

"With two feminine celebrities as patients—Gertrude and Joey—Carville never had so many chances to appear on radio and television," Stein wrote later. "In fact, at one point Dr. Jo refused to appear on any more shows because Washington might think that the [Medical Officer in Charge] had turned into a mic hog and lens louse. He insisted on clearing all requests with [Public Health Services] headquarters."

Beyond using celebrity to bring positive attention to Carville, Stein would push back against every slight, every inaccuracy. He received a note in his office at the *Star* in August 1948. One of his many far-flung correspondents had clipped and sent a letter to the editor that had run a few days before in the *Washington Evening Star*, the capital's paper of record, from a writer with the pseudonym M.M.C.

TO THE EDITOR OF THE STAR: Can't Americans express their feelings of gratitude, appreciation, and humanity without having recourse to a foolish and dangerous stunt?

Undoubtedly, the gallant little Philippine leper lady, Joey Guerrero, is deserving of our best considerations, but did we show our appreciation of her either wisely or well when we brought her over 10,000 miles by public transportation from the Philippines to the leprosarium at Carville, La.?

Hers is an "advanced case" of leprosy, according to the health officer of San Francisco and, according to him, will require many years of treatment. Such an extended and strenuous journey must have been a great strain on the patient. And what about the dozens of people who were exposed to her "advanced case" of leprosy en route? The germs of the disease are numerous in the mucus secretions. Joey's sneeze, Joey's cough would spread a shower around.

Why in the name of all that is reasonable should we bring a foreign person into this country possibly to afflict some of our own citizens with a dread disease of ancient heritage, the cure of which is very long at best, and doubtful and unreliable at worst? When will we outgrow such maudlin sentimentality?

There are many fine leprosariums in the Philippines and throughout the Pacific area equipped with the most modern facilities, and using the same advanced techniques and treatments as are used at Carville.

Would it not have been more useful to greater numbers of other sufferers if, in Joey's name, and dedicated to her for her assistance to our cause during the War, we had raised funds, and contributed it to these institutions, thus enabling them to be of more service to more patients?

I think we could have raised many thousands of dollars which, together with the thousands expended for Joey's transportation to this country would have added very substantially to the alleviation of leprosy in the Philippines.

Attorney General Clark deserves the censure of the Nation for aiding and abetting this bizarre performance. Congress would do well to inquire into his reasons for giving special permission for this outrageous undertaking—outrageous for both patient and public.

Stein called the writer of the first letter out in his own spare and brutal way, this time using Joey's story to enhance his argument.

In this enlightened day and age the ignorance and inaccuracy contained in this letter are shocking to all of us, scientists and patients, who know through research and experience, the exact facts re leprosy. Apropos Mrs. Josefina Guerrero, M.M.C.'s principal concern was that the dozens of people exposed to "Joey" en route from the Philippines might contract the disease from her sneeze or cough.

The mode of transmission of leprosy is unknown, but according to a recent statement by Dr. H. Windsor Wade, President of the International Leprosy Association and Medical Director of the Leonard Wood Memorial (The American Leprosy Foundation): "Actual observations do not support the once prevalent idea that the nasal mucous membrane is the usual portal of entry," (of the leprosy bacilli).

M.M.C. criticizes severely Attorney General Clark, for giving special permission to Joey to enter this country, even going so far as to suggest a Congressional investigation.

For M.M.C.'s correct information Attorney General Clark noted in his announcement that the United

States Public Health Service, which cooperated with the Department of Justice in investigating Joey's case had advised him that, "the chances of infection from the disease were negligible."

The U.S. P.H.S. does not base its statement on antiquated ideas or superstitions, but on years of scientific research and practical experience here at Carville.

It may interest, it will certainly instruct, M.M.C. to know that in the 54 years this hospital has cared for patients suffering from leprosy not one of the medical and nursing personnel, or employees, has ever contracted the disease. Visitors are admitted freely from 7 AM to 9 PM and are not required to take any special precautions. They mingle freely with the patients. In fact authorities are convinced that the average adult, even in endemic areas, has a natural immunity to leprosy. Further no scientist in more than 145 recorded cases has been able to infect himself or other human volunteers by attempted inoculation of the germ.

M.M.C.'s cruel and untrue letter has caused a great deal of pain to gallant little Joey Guerrero. Surely after all she did during the war for our boys, the risk of life she endured so many times, she does not deserve such misunderstanding and ingratitude as is shown in M.M.C.'s somewhat silly letter. If M.M.C. has any of the real courage of his or her convictions, such, for instance as our little Joey has shown, why not sign his or her name to the letter instead of hiding behind initials.

A man who met Joey at Tala wrote a rebuttal as well, taking the writer to task for his inaccuracies, pointing out that the transmission of Hansen's disease from one person to another is remotely communicable, "so remote that none of the American soldiers she fed during the occupation, that she led past minefields into the Battle of Manila, and those she carried, wounded, off the battlefield has been known to have contracted the disease," wrote Robert L. Zeigler. "As far as Joey is concerned, she deserves every consideration of a grateful nation for her contribution to saving the lives of our sons, and the opportunity to regain her health, nebulous as the prospects may seem."

But even the rebuttal generated fear. A writer going by C.N. relayed an old story that Stein himself had heard before, even researched: "During the winter of 1918–19 there was a leper at the Walter Reed Hospital, a United States soldier, who had contracted the disease in the Philippines. The nurse, a personal friend of mine, who attended him, was required to put on a robe, rubber gloves, and a mask when entering his room. Everything that came out of the room was sterilized. What does Mr. Zeigler mean when he states that leprosy is 'remotely communicable?' Why are there 30,000 lepers in the Philippines, according to his figures, if the disease is not readily communicable?"

Stein's response, which was verified by a nurse at Carville who knew the patient at Walter Reed: he had smallpox, not leprosy.

Stein shot letters to newspapers, magazines, business groups, advertising agencies, even to television networks that loosely used the word *leper*, as in "He's a moral leper."

"It has been said that, 'It is a gigantic task to attempt to alter a conception that people have held all over the world for many centuries, and to expect them to change suddenly, figures of speech which have long been part of the vocabulary of associations, toward which the mind turns unconsciously.' However, with due cognizance of the difficulties involved, all of which can be overcome by the cooperation of your group, we submit the following suggestion. In place of the word 'leprosy' use the word 'plague,' and replace the word 'leper' by the word 'pariah.' This rule is to apply to programs not concerned with scientific discussion of the disease but where the word is merely dragged in because it is colorful and connotative."

When patients at Carville were listening to a baseball game over the radio and heard the announcer say that if the Giants didn't win, they'd be treated like they had a compound leprosy when they returned to the Polo Grounds, off went a letter from Stanley Stein to Liberty Broadcasting in the Empire State Building.

"We realize the connotation you placed on the word leprosy is deeply imbedded in the language," he wrote to announcer Gordon McLendon. "However, we feel you would not have made the reference had you known it would offend a group or even one of your listening audience."

To Lowell Thomas from CBS radio: "The medical world is with us in our battle to outlaw this word. According to manuscript rules of the American Medical Association, the word 'leper' can not be used in any of its publications."

To Morgan Beatty from NBC's *News of the World*: "The nearly four hundred patients of this hospital, the Nation's only Continental Leprosarium, bitterly resent being classed with Russian spies and communists, especially some of us who are veterans of both world wars."

And almost always, he would include a gift subscription to the *Star*, or at least a few issues, so the offending party could see the people they'd hurt. More often than not, Stein received thoughtful, genuine responses from those he took to task.

"I humbly apologize to the patients in your hospital for what might seem to be an affront to them," wrote US representative Karl Mundt, from South Dakota, who had suggested on the House floor that Communists were mental lepers. "While my reference was made in the sense of the Biblical references to leprosy, I want to assure you that I feel nothing but the deepest sympathy for those people who have contracted Hansen's disease. Please be assured that in the future I shall be more careful in my analogies."

The third front in Stein's campaign would be mass education, and on this front he began growing the circulation of his newsletter. A field representative for the American Legion who had taken an interest in Carville suggested Stein print the mimeographed *Star* like a magazine. The state commander of the Forty and Eight, the American Legion's fun and honor society, decided to buy the *Star* a press, type, and all the necessities. The Louisiana delegation of the American Legion convinced the other states at a national meeting to adopt the *Star* as a national project, and the new subscriptions after that overwhelmed the presses to the point that the Forty and Eight in New York bought Carville a flatbed press, a paper cutter, and a folding machine. Someone else gave them a mechanical stitcher, and someone else secured a linotype machine. The hospital turned over an addressograph and the US government put in place salaries for more staffers. Soon Stein and his cohorts were turning out fourteen thousand copies of the *Star* every month, sending them to public libraries, doctors' offices, medical schools, and homes in the United States and sixty-eight foreign countries.

"We may not be a determining factor in changing the archaic attitude of people toward Hansen's disease," Stein wrote, "but we have at least been a catalytic agent."

44

FENCES

After a short stay in her temporary room, Joey moved into a boardinghouse on campus that required a feat of housekeeping to make it livable. She lacked the modern amenities and knick-knacks that make a home, but room 200 in house 19-2 would do. The walls were painted pastel green. The floor was tiled with beige linoleum bearing a fern design. Her windowsills were covered by potted houseplants, and two bookshelves were filled with books, as was her bed. At night, she moved the books to the floor. A chest of drawers with a mirror stood against the wall facing her bed, and to the side was a cabinet, which held her two-plate burner. In one corner was a hanging pot with ivy. The walls were decorated with photographs of her many friends, but dominant on the wall was her favorite picture of the Sacred Heart. Her writing desk was pushed near the window, and on it sat a new Underwood portable type-writer, a gift from the Underwood Corporation in New York, which sent along a message with it: "It seemed very appropriate that our message be in the form of an article that would prove useful for many years to come. We would like to present Mrs. Guerrero with an Underwood typewriter with best wishes and appreciation for the great work she has done."

She put it to good use. It took her weeks to respond to the letters that had piled up, but she worked at it diligently until every piece of correspondence had been dealt with, including letters from both Rene and Cynthia. Cynthia asked for a carriage for her doll, but Joey wasn't allowed to leave the campus, so she had to find someone who could help her. She missed Cynthia dearly.

"I love that baby of mine," she wrote to a friend. "I felt like I could give up anything but not her. Then, separation meant something like death."

She soon fell into a routine. She woke to an alarm before sunrise, before most of the patients had started to stir. She thought of it as the gong sounding to mark the beginning of the battle between flesh and spirit. She hurried to the chapel for early Mass every day, and every day she was glad she did. After Mass she would hustle back to her room to make the bed and tidy up and write a few letters before the breakfast bell rang at 7:30 AM. Some days she made coffee and toast in her room, but most often she joined the rest of the nearly four hundred patients in the cafeteria. School started at 8:30; she was trying to get an American high school diploma. The lunch bell rang at 11:00, then she went back to school until 3:15 PM. In the afternoon, she played badminton or visited with friends or pushed a twenty-three-year-old invalid named Mabel around the campus in her wheelchair, trying to lift the girl's spirits. She also began reading to the blind patients and those who had never learned how. She preferred nonfiction and loved biographies and books on travel.

Her job at the *Star* paid a modest salary, and she had begun to save up to buy a radio-phonograph she saw in a catalog priced at $179. The jazz everyone at Carville seemed to enjoy so much was grating. She preferred Mozart over Miles Davis. She liked listening to her music more than anything.

"I love music, although I do not play any instrument, nor can I read even one note," she wrote to a reporter for the *Catholic Digest*. "Yet, I can sit for hours listening to the music of the masters. One of my secret ambitions is to be able to go to all the places where I can listen to music: Carnegie Hall, for example, the Metropolitan, Hollywood Bowl."

She enjoyed styling hair and giving the other patients permanents. She also loved making clothes and wrote to a fashion academy in New York, asking if she could take a home-study course. The school asked for references, so Joey sent back a few newspaper clippings.

"I didn't want to bother anyone with this, so I just sent them a few newspaper clippings about me," she told a friend. "I thought this would establish my identity."

The academy wrote back: "Because of your wonderful service to your own government as well as that of the United States, we are extending to you a scholarship in the Home Study Division through the Emil Alvin Hartman foundation. Therefore, we are returning your payment herewith."

From then on, she worked to design clothing and studied the history of fashion. She read every book she could get her hands on about how to sketch costumes and then carry them out. She started making her own clothes and designing dresses for the other patients. She spent hours bent over her Singer sewing machine, and her efforts were amateurish at first. It took her three weeks to make herself a floral-print dress. But she was getting the hang of it. Her desire was to leave the hospital with an array of practical skills so she could easily find employment once she was on her own. She knew two languages. She was learning how to be a journalist. She could type and practiced the skill by volunteering as secretary for the Patients Federation. Not a day went by without at least one of the other patients approaching her to ask if she would mind filling out a form or answering a letter. "Just tell them I was glad to hear from them and that I'm alright," they would instruct her.

In the same vein, she spent as much time as she could in the manual arts department of the hospital learning carpentry. She built herself a desk, sanding and staining it until it was handsome. The work wasn't foreign, for she recalled building coffins for the dead at Tala so they'd be buried in something more respectable than a burlap sack or straw mat.

Beyond that, she seemed to always be hosting visitors to campus, some of them old friends and some of them starstruck strangers who just wanted to meet the little Filipina they had read about.

"Louisiana is overlooking a new source for tax revenue and the state has been most astute in its levying of taxes," wrote a reporter for the *Star*. "But if they would just charge toll to each of the visitors who brave the gravel path from Baton Rouge to visit Joey they could promise two chickens for every pot."

Father Fred Zimmerman, who used to bring Joey chocolate bars at Tala, came with a fellow priest and stayed for two days. Father Walter Debold of Saint Joseph's Church in Jersey City, who also used to visit Tala when he was stationed in the islands with the 248th Station Hospital, flew two thousand miles to say hello. Father Fred Julien, who remembered the lady in black outside the Ateneo de Manila, drove over from his new parish in Lufkin, Texas, three times to visit with Joey. Elsie Voigt, who was a field auditor for UNRRA in Manila and was introduced to Joey by Frank Gaines, also made time to visit.

"Once upon a time I thought there was no such thing as a true friend," Joey wrote. "I was mistaken."

One day she walked into the doctor's office at the hospital, and there stood Brig. Gen. Howard Smith, assistant surgeon general in charge of public health work for the United States in the Far East. He had served as MacArthur's medical chief and escaped Bataan with President Manuel Roxas and was among the small delegation that raised the flag at Corregidor when the United States reclaimed the island. He spread his arms and gave Joey a massive hug.

"Let me look at you," he said. "How are you, child?"

They'd first met through Frank Gaines when Joey was at Tala and she had given the general some spare fishing equipment. They saw each other many times after that, and Smith had vouched for Joey's war record when she was trying to get her passport. He promised to visit her when he was in the States. She had met several generals, but he was her favorite.

She had a special talent for leading tours of the giant campus with its tennis courts, library, movie house, and some three miles of covered walkways leading from building to building. The Patients Federation and the staff of the *Star* had convinced the medical officer in charge in 1946 to lift the restriction on visitors. He had admitted it wasn't because of danger of contact but just to protect patients from the morbidly curious. He agreed to change the rule if the *Star* staff promised to assume the responsibility of conducting visitors through the hospital. Since then, thousands had come, many to see Joey, and thousands had left with their minds changed about Hansen's disease. The former mayor of Richmond, Michigan, who toured Carville, promised to help in the educational campaign by giving talks about Hansen's disease to civic clubs.

"I visited your Marine Hospital last month and Joey's tour around the place did something for me," wrote Vince Pizzolato of Plaquemine, Louisiana. "I feel that you should solicit visitors from nearby communities and really educate them on Hansen's disease. Here's a few subscriptions from a group of my friends to your paper."

When her visitors called her a hero, Joey buckled and tried to correct them. "I am just a simple, ordinary person, not a heroine," she wrote to one admirer. "I did only what you or any other would have done if called upon to do so. I was fortunate, for to me was given that which was not given to those more worthy. God chose a weak and fragile vessel of clay of the poorest quality when He chose me, but such are the ways of God—they are strange to us poor mortals."

She started a column for the *Star* called Jottings by Joey, where she kept readers informed about whatever charitable act she was up to. She also kept up the struggle to help the patients at Tala. One of the first improvements Joey had sparked at the colony was a nursery for babies born to patients. Before, the newborns were simply taken by the government and placed in orphanages, never to be seen again by their parents. A group of Franciscan nuns had volunteered to care for the babies at a newly built nursery, and parents could at least see their children through a partition. But after Joey arrived at Carville, she received a letter from one of the nuns saying the government was threatening to shut down the nursery unless money could be raised to expand the facility and provide better clothing and medical equipment. Joey immediately began writing letters to anybody she could think of, friend or stranger, asking for help. She wrote to a steel magnate in Pennsylvania, an heiress in New York, and an oil man in Texas, pleading for donations. The contributions rolled in from all over, from Sister M. Florella's Xavier High Group in Phoenix, Arizona, and from Bishop Fulton Sheen and from Father Haggerty's group in Springfield, Illinois. A check for $1,000 came from Mrs. Betty Burdette, national president of the American Legion Auxiliary. Joey didn't know how much it would take to keep the nursery open, but she did everything she could to help.

Once a friend wrote to her asking, "What can I send you to help you pass the time, something you really need?" In jest, Joey wrote back, "We don't pass time here at the hospital, time passes us."

She was convinced she could be cured but had no idea how long that might take.

"The doctors do not know how long I may have to stay, but of course I cannot leave until I am well, or have passed the 12 negative tests—three years, four, five, who knows?" she wrote to a man named Edward Harrigan. "Everything rests with God and science. I cannot speak of the treatments, as I do not know if I am allowed to do that. However, I feel that everything is being done for me: there is a sense of solidarity about this place. The medical staff are competent and highly efficient. The sister nurses are class A; they are always gentle, solicitous, kind, and very human. However, I think the secret lies in cooperation. There must be a coordination and cooperation between doctor and patient. In this way, I believe treatment can be a success. This is true of all things, isn't it?"

When she was alone, she wrote poetry, her hobby. Much of it was religious, hymnlike exaltations of almighty God or Mother

Mary. Some of it revealed the cultured environment in which she had been raised. Some spoke to the yearning she felt to be on the other side of the Carville barbed wire, to be able to see and experience the best the world had to offer.

Wunderlust

I went globe-trotting across the hemisphere—
In quest of gold, frankincense and myrrh.
I traveled through many a town and city,
In curious pursuit of art and things of beauty.
I browsed among the masters at the Louvre—
Took in the fashion shows and even the Follies Bergere!
I thrilled to the gory bullfights in gay Spain,
And for a constitutional, a stroll on the Rue de la Paix!
I sat in ecstatic rapture at the Scala in Milan,
Loved and lived a lifetime with Puccini's Cho-Cho-San.
Paris in the springtime, I had a rendezvous with Mona Lisa,
Her smile mocked at me like the leaning Tower of Pisa.
Curiosity for Farrouk took me to Biarritz and Monte Carlo—
I'll take a Bergman anytime and the luscious Greta Garbo!
The season found me applauding Sadler Well's Margot Fonteyn,
For unparalleled delight, give me the Dying Swan again!
I heard the Tower of London's twelve o'clock chime,
In Paris, I'd be having café au lait for an American dime.
The bitter taste of fog, the cold and mist I could not stand,
Give me warm Manhattan, roller coasters on Coney Island!
Shades of Louisiana lay among derricks of troubled Iran—
And painted deserts in the sky in Sweden's Midnight Sun!
Restless hearts smoldered in once-happy Yugoslavia,
Even peace got lost at St. Sophia's in Czechoslovakia.
On a pilgrimage to Portugal, I knelt before a shrine,
Out there I was told the angels have a whale of a time!
A tour included a mountain climb to the famous Matterhorn,

Terra firma for me, I like my feet on solid ground.
Like many countries, France has the great River Seine,
Across her span the Bridge of Sighs all over again.
Germany has her Rhine, through Italy's valleys, the River Po.
Nostalgic memories of muddy Mississippi follow wherever I go!
At last I stood in reverent awe before a saintly man,
His frail body in raiment white, his lean face lined and wan—
Before him all of Europe's grandeur faded into bliss,
As I knelt down to receive his blessing of peace.
Home holds enchantment no matter where you roam—
In any time or clime, there is no place like home!
Old yearnings weave a magic spell in this happy sphere—
For here I shall find gold, frankincense, and myrrh!

She did not curse or gamble or drink, and she only smoked when offered, to be polite. She went to Mass every day and knelt in the same spot in the Catholic chapel, praying to be clean.

Two years, three years, four. Treatments, physicals, sulfone shots. Brahms, Tchaikovsky, Beethoven. Letters, letters, and more letters, which she closed with prayers and signed "Your little friend, Joey."

"I cannot speak of the future too much. I do not know what God has in store for me, or what He wills of me," she wrote to a man inquiring about her plans after Carville. "Whatever He desires, I desire; whatever He wills, I will. If it is His desire that I never get well, and die here, to lie beneath the brown sod under the Louisiana skies would not be bad. And as long as I live, no matter what, provided that my life is a fitting Calvary, and I a fitting instrument to bring millions of hearts to Him, who is the true reason for my being, what else have I to wish for? I only ask that I love him with all my heart, all the days of my life, that I remain forever pleasing and beautiful in His sight. That is all I ask, nothing more. I accept, and as He desires, He will give to me the graces to carry, as He has given to me to carry on with joy and peace of heart. Some day, my boat will come and carry me to the home I have longed for and dreamed of."

45

WALK ALONE

The sizzling storm clouds rolled in low over the swamp, and lightning cut the sky and threw short, sharp flashes of brilliance down on the oak trees dotting the campus of the US Public Health Service Hospital in Carville. Thunder rattled the windows of the building that housed the auditorium, which was filling with folks from all over, shaking off the rain, taking their seats to watch the commencement.

Two patients were graduating—Joey, the valedictorian, and Bert King, an eighteen-year-old from Florida, salutatorian by default. Newsmen arrived early—Hugh Milligan from the Associated Press, Ed Clinton from the Baton Rouge *State-Times*, Charles Pierce from the *Times-Picayune* in New Orleans. The Baton Rouge WJBO's Brooks Reed taped a fifteen-minute interview with Joey, which would air nationally on Morgan Beatty's *World News Roundup*. Philippines consul general Benjamin T. Tirona was ushered in. A former chief nurse from the Fourth General Hospital in Manila, Miss Elizabeth Simon, who had met Joey after liberation, drove down from Ohio. They all called Joey their friend and meant it.

Sister Laura Stricker banged out "Pomp and Circumstance" on the piano. The stage was decorated with fresh flowers, and the resident chaplains, Rev. Edward Boudreaux and Rev. Carl Elder, offered the invocation and benediction. Dr. John W. Melton, pas-

Joey Guerrero poses before her graduation at Carville, Louisiana, in July 1953.
National Hansen's Disease Museum, Stanley Stein Archives Collection, NHDM-1930

tor of the First Presbyterian Church in Baton Rouge, handled the
commencement.

Joey was up onstage wearing a white cap and gown, smiling,
throwing little waves when she spotted someone in the crowd she
recognized. An old man slowly sipped on a bottle of beer in the
canteen, watching the hubbub. He remembered his own graduation
thirty-five years before, just before he contracted leprosy and was
sent, or sentenced, to Carville. Stanley Stein was in the audience,
too, dark glasses over his eyes but looking proud nonetheless.

Joey was thirty-six now. She had worked for four years toward
this night, and it had come with the requisite chaos that defined her
life. The day before, she was scheduled to participate in a "deportation hearing" held at Carville by the US Immigration and Naturalization Service. The same government that had cut tape to extend
a welcome to the woman who helped the country win a war was
now in the process of trying to eject her. Joey's visa had expired, and

without help from someone in the bureaucracy, she would be sent back to the Philippines, which was still trying to recover from the war and still dealing with a violent Huk insurgency. On the bright side, by July 1953 her health had improved dramatically. Dr. Johansen had been having great success with the sulfones—Diasone, Promacetin, and sulphetrorie. The doctor, who had just retired after twenty-nine years at Carville, knew the drugs could cure secondary infections and halt the spread of leprosy. When he first arrived at Carville, many thought there was no hope for a cure. But he knew that now, if the disease was caught in its early stages, a patient could get treatment with sulfones for two or three years at Carville, then be discharged without any disfigurement. After that, treatment was outpatient. Joey's classmate, Bert Wood, was an example of that. He arrived in Carville two years before without any of the telltale disfigurement that typically accompanied Hansen's disease. And he was slated to be discharged after the graduation ceremony, thanks in large part to the hard work of Dr. Jo.

In fact, Dr. Jo was responsible for the visitors there to see Joey graduate. It was he who had thrown open the doors to guests. The hospital now had a softball team, and they played in an open league in Baton Rouge. Patients were allowed to visit their homes twice a year and stay for a month.

"In days now gone, the best word we could give the new patient was one of possibility or chance that his condition would not become worse," Dr. Johansen wrote in an editorial in the *Star*. "For some—many still young—Carville was the end of the road. But, today, we can talk with some degree of confidence about the hope of recovery and rehabilitation, provided the patient receives prompt and proper medical attention and continues his medication. Now, we may think of the treatment period at Carville as we regard the time spent under care for any other illness that requires longer than usual hospitalization."

The advances against the disease in the past ten years had been swift and accurate, and they dovetailed with Stanley Stein's public relations campaign to enlighten the country. His thousands of letters were paying off. Old superstitions were on their way out. Even Harry Truman took note.

"My congratulations to THE STAR on its Tenth Anniversary," the president had written to Stein. "I know that it has consistently carried out its objective—radiating the light of truth on Hansen's disease. Steady progress is being made in dissipating public fear of this disease, so that those afflicted by it can lead more normal and happier lives. It is important, of course, to get rid of Hansen's disease altogether. Because medical science is making such remarkable progress, it is reasonable to believe that this can be done. I am certainly glad to note in the pages of THE STAR that a new method of treatment is proving effective. THE STAR deserves full credit for contributing to a better understanding of Hansen's disease."

One example of the changing attitudes among the general public came in 1949, a year after Joey arrived at Carville. The sulfones worked on Gertrude Hornbostel, as she predicted, and the disease was arrested. She and Hans decided to move to New York. And the move was made void of the expected controversy. A short story ran on page 11 of the *New York Times*, prompted by Major Hornbostel himself, who issued a statement to the press, an appeal for understanding.

"For years my wife and I have fought to enlighten the people. Our only medium has been through the press. Leper and leprosy are words that should be stricken from our language, as the doctors have already done," his statement said. "Of course, the trouble lies with popular superstition, ignorance and fear that goes back to Biblical times. Those who have Hansen's disease today and who have the wherewithal to buy the new sulfone drugs are far better off than if they had any other disease I know of but unfortunately these same people will suffer mentally until the people of the United States appreciate what this disease really means."

Gertrude, too, kept up her activism and had several letters to the editor published in the *Times*.

T. H. Richard, a writer on staff at the *Star*, noted the importance of the convergence of Joey and the Hornbostels at Carville, writing that the "chain of circumstances" had led to "rewriting the dialogue for the roles played by the general public in Hansen's disease."

"The Major brought Hansen's disease into the headlines of American newspapers by announcing his desire to continue living with his wife," he wrote. "Joey came to this country to become a patient at Carville and added her bit to the increasing favorable publicity that is shaking the superstitious outlook on Hansen's disease to its roots."

Life inside the fence had improved by leaps as the fear faded. The Louisiana legislature removed "leprosy" from the category of quarantinable diseases like smallpox and yellow fever, and state workers laid blacktop over the fifteen-mile stretch of gravel road that led from Baton Rouge to the hospital. A new book about Carville, written by a former patient, was making waves and had been condensed and published by *Reader's Digest*. Millions of listeners heard Joey tell her story on the CBS *We, the People* broadcast, and newspapers across the country carried glowing reports about the "fascinating and unusual" program. "When the facts about Hansen's disease and the activities of Carville patients reach the attentive ears of some 10,000,000 listeners and the watchful eyes of 1,000,000 simultaneously, then we really are going places," Ann Page wrote in the *Star*.

Joey cut the ribbon that formally opened the hospital's plush new Club Lounge, a gift from Mrs. John F. Tims of New Orleans. The same big-city socialites who had worked so hard at historical preservation in the French Quarter found a new target for their charity up the Mississippi River at Carville. The patients held a Christmas party sponsored by the Women's Activities Club of the Louisiana Southern Bell Telephone and Telegraph Company, and they opened gifts donated by the Campbell Soup Company in Chicago. The guard at the gate counted 366 visitors who turned out for the celebration. The American Legion Auxiliary donated another station wagon for use at Carville, their fourth. The Louisiana Voyageurs sponsored a bicycle drive and gave a bike to every patient who wanted one. Lake Johansen, named after Dr. Jo because it was his pet project for years, opened on campus and was stocked with fish. The patients were soon having fishing rodeos and speedboat regattas. The recreation department organized a golf tournament on the nine-hole course on campus, and the American Legion Auxiliary sent seventy-five homemade cakes for the occasion. They celebrated Mardi Gras with an extravagant parade and ball. Orchestras and theater troupes were now making stops in Carville to perform, and Joey wrote reviews of the performances for the *Star*. The beautiful Broadway and Hollywood actress Tallulah Bankhead had taken a keen interest in Stanley Stein. She pestered her high-society friends in New York to subscribe to the *Star* and often wrote notes of encouragement, which Stein printed in the magazine as "Tallulahgrams." "My darling Stanley and all the wonderful people at Carville," one read. "May I extend my deepest appreciation, love and congratulations to you and your co-workers on your tenth anniversary with THE STAR. It has deeply interested me, as you know, and so many of my friends. Thank you for having enlightened us."

Perhaps the biggest event, or the most symbolic, was when men removed the strands of barbed wire atop the fence ringing the campus.

And now the auditorium was filling for the first formal school commencement exercises in the fifty-nine years the hospital had been open. At first they wouldn't let Joey take classes. She had wanted to enroll in a college correspondence course in journalism but lacked the appropriate high school credits in the States. The school at the hospital, which opened in 1949, was reserved for the younger patients. She eventually talked her way into class.

"My first day at school was uncomfortable, both for myself as well as the others," she wrote in the *Star*. "The boys were shy at having someone considerably older than they were in the classes, and I was shy because everyone else seemed like a child to me."

As the days went by, though, everyone relaxed. Joey started to feel like a child again, stimulated by the schoolwork and the companionship of much younger students, all full of curiosity. She made straight As and completed all the required courses.

At the graduation ceremony, a representative for Louisiana governor Robert Kennon presented Joey with a letter of congratulations from the chief of state. A petition circulated in the audience, pleading with the president of the United States to help Joey gain permanent residency and citizenship. A national radio program mentioned the effort as part of a newscast.

When it was her turn to give the valedictory address, Joey walked to the microphone, smiling. "It has not been easy," she said. "I have often been discouraged. I was sick. I was tired. I was disgusted. And there were moments when everything seemed wrong and without purpose. But I told myself that I cannot live forever on the charity of my friends. I must stand on my own two feet. But how? With crutches? With stilts? With leanings? No. I must learn to walk alone."

She had in mind the days ahead, when the drugs had done their work and when her tests came back negative for leprosy each month over the course of a year. She'd be cleared, and she would be given the freedom to choose her own course.

"What if I should leave the hospital suddenly? What, I asked myself, could I do?"

46

PRAISE

On August 24, 1953, *Time* published a letter from its publisher, updating readers on the heroine who was the centerpiece of the magazine's July 19, 1948, story that generated more than four thousand letters to the editor, the vast majority expressing sympathy and interest in Joey's future.

> By now most people have probably forgotten the story of a frail heroine from the Philippines named Josefina ("Joey") Guerrero. After the Japanese invaded the Philippines, Joey became a guerrilla; when the Americans landed on Leyte in World War II, Joey continued to be a US spy, flitting back & forth across the Japanese lines, carrying messages, maps, food, clothes. She had a sure immunity from capture: her face and body were blotched with the sores of leprosy, of which the Japanese soldiers were morbidly fearful.

The publisher had received a letter from Joey herself, a short note expressing personal triumph: "Dear Mr. Linen. This is it! I thought you might like to know that I made it! I wanted you to rejoice with me."

She was graduating from high school, she told him. He asked a *Time* correspondent named Ed Clinton to head to Carville and check on her, to send a report on Joey's school career and her graduation.

> On her graduation day, reported Clinton, Joey was no longer wan and nervous. Treatment had brought her disease almost to the arrested point, and only a few pocked scars remained. Dressed in a white cap and gown, she mounted the steps to the stage of the hospital auditorium to make the valedictory address to some 400 fellow patients and friends, including the Philippine consul from New Orleans.
>
> Joey told her story with simple feeling. The last five years had not been easy ones. Shortly after her arrival at Carville, her illness was complicated by an attack of double pneumonia.

Many years had passed since her days in the convent school in Manila. The return to studies, as Joey expressed, was not easy, but she had finished and she wanted her friends to know.

> After four years of such investing, Joey collected her due interest: an accredited high-school diploma. She also landed a job as one of the paid, part-time staff members of the *Star*, the community news magazine. Now, Joey hopes to study shorthand, bookkeeping, and journalism. She also hopes to achieve her greatest ambition: permanent residence in the U.S. and U.S. citizenship.
>
> In recent weeks that hope has been shadowed by the possibility of deportation, since her temporary visa has expired. Last year two special bills to grant her citizenship died in committee when the 82nd Congress adjourned. And a fortnight ago, an Immigration Service

official ordered Joey to leave the country, but gave her
the privilege of voluntary departure. Last week, however,
Joey's future was brightened again. Immigration officials
in Washington promised that no action toward her deportation would be taken for several months. That will give
Congress time to consider another private bill granting
her permanent U.S. residence.

47

BUREAUCRACY

There's a fine chance that a glitch in the great American system of governance was solely to blame for the regular, soulless letters arriving at Carville for Mrs. Josefina V. Guerrero from the US Immigration and Naturalization Service (INS), informing said leprosy patient and war hero that her temporary visa had expired and she was no longer welcome on American soil, that she should voluntarily depart the United States at once.

There were several problems for Joey when she received the letters. The first was the stress. She was still receiving treatments, and the thought of being kicked out of the country by a bureaucrat with a clipboard put her health in jeopardy. She hated the thought, hated the worry that seemed to hover over her head. The second problem was that she had nothing to return to in the Philippines. Although that was the plan originally, the letters had slowed and then stopped, and she had fallen so far out of contact with Rene and Cynthia, as ostracized as she was, that going back home lacked appeal. They had moved on with their lives, and she had moved on with hers, even to the point of dating other patients. Cynthia, in her late teens now, did not know her mother. As painful as it was, Joey had become something entirely different since she left home. Part of that transformation was learning how to survive and even thrive in a place of possible permanence. Even with the success of the sulfone drugs, none of the patients knew for sure that they'd ever be released. They could hope. Meanwhile they had to learn to exist inside an insular world behind the fence. Joey would see Cynthia again, one last time, but the two were strangers and the meeting would be awkward and short and leave the daughter with burning questions about the mother—questions with no answers.

Joey had decided she wanted to try to stay in America, so her friends went to work. Rep. James Morrison, a Democrat from Louisiana whom she had never met in person, introduced a bill in the House to either grant Joey citizenship or grant her permanent residence in the United States. It was the shortest of bills.

> Be it enacted by the Senate and House of Representatives of the United States of America in Congress assembled, that Josefina V. Guerrero shall be held and considered to be, and is hereby, unconditionally admitted to the character, rights, and privileges of a citizen of the United States.

Sen. Herbert H. Lehman, a Democrat from New York, introduced a similar bill in the Senate.

"A number of my constituents have expressed great interest in the passage of your bill," Rep. Richard Bolling, a Democrat from Missouri, wrote to Lehman. "If there is any way in which you feel I may be helpful in this matter I am at your service."

Even with support, both bills stalled in committee, which is what sometimes happens, even with legislation with the best of intentions. Morrison, undeterred, introduced another.

When her friends outside of Carville learned of the mess, they began organizing on her behalf. The American Legion passed a resolution offering their support and promising to petition the INS. Their letter-writing campaign reached more than twenty members of congress. "As a matter of fact, there have been so many letters in Joey's behalf addressed to myself and the committee that they are far too numerous to record in the Congressional Record," James Morrison wrote.

Joey had great hope it would all be over by Christmas of 1953. "It isn't the burdens and difficulties along the road of life which makes it discouraging or heartbreaking for the yoke is made lighter when others extend a helping hand to ease the weight from one's shoulder," she wrote in the *Star*. "It is a constant source of wonder and amazement to me the way people everywhere have given of their time and effort to make my yoke sweet."

The "Joey Campaign" was especially encouraging. Led by the Baton Rouge Business and Professional Women's Club, it aimed to generate unprecedented letters in support of Joey. A simple mailing was passed around, and members were encouraged to make copies and spread it throughout their own networks.

Subject: "JOEY"—Mrs. Josefina Guerrero

* * * * * * * * * *

Mrs. Guerrero, a native of the Philippines, is now a patient at the United States Public Health Service Hospital at Carville, Louisiana. During World War II, she gained international recognition for her acts of heroism as an underground agent in the Japanese-held Philippines and for her invaluable assistance to the United States Army during the period of invasion. She accomplished many daring and courageous missions, such as the smuggling of food, messages, and medicine to United States prisoners of war, the mapping of enemy fortifications for our Air Force, and, on one occasion, by walking 56 miles through enemy lines to report a mine field where the United States 37th Division was scheduled to attack Manila.

As a token of appreciation for these accomplish-ments, the United States Government awarded Mrs. Guerrero the Medal of Freedom with Silver Palm, the highest award given to any civilian for services rendered to this country during the time of war. Cardinal Spellman presented to her a Medallion in recognition of "Christian fortitude and concern for fellow sufferers."

In July 1948 she gained admittance to this country on a temporary visitor's permit under the Ninth Proviso to Section Three of the act of February 5, 1917, for treatment of Hansen's disease (leprosy) at Carville. Her admission was subsequently extended to August 20, 1951. In order that she might receive additional treatment for her disease, and, on or about the same time, a private bill was introduced in Congress, seeking to grant her citizenship in the United States. This bill, **HR 2412**, is still pending in the House of Representatives. Meanwhile, a hearing on Mrs. Guerrero's case was held July 31, 1953, and it was decided that under immigration laws, she must be deported. This decision has been appealed, and the US Board of Immigration Appeals will eventually pass on the question of her deportation. It is, therefore, essential that **HR 2412** be passed at the earliest date possible. The American Legion, at its national Convention in St. Louis in August 1953, and the Louisiana Federation of Business and Professional Women's Clubs in August of 1953, passed resolutions opposing the deportation of Mrs. Guerrero.

Those who have come to know Mrs. Guerrero and her situation feel that she justly deserves to remain in the United States. Not only did she give her invaluable service to our country during the war; today she is making an outstanding contribution as a living symbol of the hopefulness for ultimate recovery by all Hansen's disease patients. As a result of the attention which her case has brought to the hospital at Carville, thousands of persons have gained a better understanding of the disease and its treatment. Mrs. Guerrero has been a most cooperative and industrious patient, and this is best exemplified by her successful completion of the high school courses presented at the hospital. She gives of her time to fellow patients in many ways, such as reading to the blind, setting patients' hair, and by means of her own pleasing and cheerful personality, making life brighter for others around the hospital.

* * * * * * * * * *

What YOU can do:
(1) Write to your Congressman immediately, urging passage of **HR 2412**.
(2) Send this material to a friend, asking her or him to share in our effort by sending it on to another.
(3) Give this information to your local newspaper.
(4) Adopt the suggested Resolution on the reverse side.

**LET'S KEEP THIS LETTER MOVING FOR
"JOEY"
For Additional Copies Write "JOEY CAMPAIGN",
2159 Tulip, Baton Rouge, La.**

RESOLUTION
(Suggested)
WHEREAS, Mrs. Josefina Guerrero was awarded the Medal of Freedom with Silver Palm, the highest award the United States Government can give to a civilian for battle services to this country, for her heroic activities during the Japanese occupation and the American invasion of the Philippines; and,

WHEREAS, Mrs. Guerrero was admitted to the United States on July 2, 1948, for treatment of Hansen's disease at the US Public Health Service Hospital, Carville, Louisiana; and,

WHEREAS, Mrs. Guerrero has faced periodic deportation hearings since the expiration of her visa on August 20, 1951; and,

WHEREAS, a private bill (H.R. 2412) is presently pending in Congress, directed toward granting permanent residence to Mrs. Guerrero; and,

WHEREAS, the passage of this bill will allow Mrs. Guerrero to remain in the United States for further treatment which she needs and grant her a reward she justly deserves; now, therefore,

BE IT RESOLVED, that _____ _____ Club go on record as opposing deportation of Mrs. Guerrero.

BE IT FURTHER RESOLVED, that a copy of this resolution be forwarded to your congressmen.

Joey also had an attorney working on her behalf, pro bono. Robert Kleinpeter of Baton Rouge was a tireless advocate, and he kept in close contact with Rep. James Morrison. She also had the press on her side: James Linen from *Time* and Frank Folsom of RCA. Nixon Denton of the Cincinnati *Times-Star*, who was with the First Cavalry Division that saved the prisoners at Santo Tomas, wrote a full column calling on the Thirty-Seventh Division Association "not to boot its chance to smooth the way for Joey."

"Can any gift equal his desire to help me?" Joey wrote in a column in the *Star*. "There is no gift like it, even at Tiffany's."

On December 21, 1953, just before Christmas, the legendary Broadway producer and syndicated columnist Billy Rose, who had never before met Joey, took up the cause like so many others before. Newspapers from Montana to Maine carried his Pitching Horseshoes column about Joey:

During the last seven years I've written more than 1,000 columns—about 1,000,000 words—and I have never used one of these words to ask anybody to write or wire his congressman about anything.

Today, however, I'm going to urge my readers—and their sisters, cousins, and aunts—to get in touch with their senators and representatives on behalf of a Philippine woman named Josefina Guerrero who wants to become a citizen of the United States.

Who is Josefina Guerrero? Well, if you haven't already read it in one of the national magazines, here's her story.

In 1941 Josefina, called "Joey" by her friends, was 23 years old, married to a medical student in Manila, and mother of a 2-year-old daughter named Cynthia. One day her doctor noticed a strange blotch on her body and, after a series of tests, told her she had leprosy and advised her to leave her home at once. Joey packed and left that night.

When the Japs landed in Manila in 1942, they took over the hospital in which Joey was being treated and turned her and the other patients into the street. A few days later she was attacked by two drunken Japanese soldiers, but beat them off with such frenzy that a member of the Philippine underground who witnessed the incident asked if she'd like to join up.

For the next two years, despite her aching head and blotchy skin, Joey smuggled in food and medicine to American internees and prisoners of war, and smuggled out military information which the guerrillas in the hills radioed to Australia.

When our troops landed on Leyte, it was Joey who mapped the Japanese fortifications on the Manila waterfront and their anti-aircraft batteries along Dewey Boulevard. These maps she managed to get through to her underground contacts by concealing them in hollowed-out apples and oranges. She was, of course, stopped many times by Japanese sentries, but when they saw her lacerated face and swollen hands they drew back in fear and let her pass.

Early in 1945 when the 37th infantry division was blasting its way into Manila, Joey took her most dangerous job. The Japanese had mined and booby-trapped an area through which the allied forces had to pass and a detailed map of the danger spots had to be delivered to division headquarters 40 miles north of the capital. Joey volunteered to walk the 40 miles through the Japanese lines.

En route, time after time, the Japanese questioned her, but her mauled face was her passport. Twice Joey was arrested but, thanks to her sores, got away. And when she finally reached American headquarters, the map taped between her shoulder blades, she was too sick to eat the pancakes they made for her.

Shortly after the armistice, the United States war department awarded Joey the Medal of Freedom with Silver Palm, one of the highest decorations it can bestow on an alien. In 1948 she received something even more important to her—a temporary visa to enter the United States, and permission to go to the leprosarium at Carville, La.

At Carville, Joey was treated with the new sulfone drugs and, as of today, the disease is completely arrested in her. Her head no longer aches, she can eat normally again, and there are only a few scars on her face.

Early this year the United States immigration service informed Joey that her visa had expired and she would have to be deported. The officials were sympathetic but—well, the law was the law.

Moved by her story, Representative James H. Morrison of Louisiana introduced a bill to grant her citizenship, and persuaded the immigration authorities to let her remain until the measure came up. Unfortunately, the bill died in committee. However, it will be introduced again by the Louisiana legislator when congress convenes next month, and a similar bill, I understand, will be submitted to the senate.

So far, so good—but bills, even the best of them, have a way of getting lost on Capitol Hill.

This is where you and I come in. As soon as I have finished this piece, I'm going to wire senators and congressmen who represent my district in New York.

And, at the risk of sounding like a professional do-gooder, I urge you to give Joey the break she rates and do a bit of wiring or writing yourself. In your words or mine, here's what I'd suggest you say: "I think Josefina Guerrero, one of our top spies in the war against Japan, should be permitted to remain in the United States. Please do your best to expedite the bill introduced by Representative James H. Morrison of Louisiana, which will come before the judiciary committee when Congress convenes."

48

SISTERS

Joey and Ann Page stood together outside the closed doors of the Protestant chapel at Carville on a Sunday in October 1954. A cold front had blown in, and there was a nip in the air as they nervously whispered outside the Mission Revival–style church. Inside, twenty sisters of the Beta Sigma Phi sorority were busy preparing for a ceremony. They poured punch and unveiled a chocolate cake with icing that said WELCOME SISTERS.

Joey and Ann, who had reclaimed her birth name, Annabel Guidry, were both being installed as members of the international chapter of Beta Sigma Phi, a cultural, social, and service sorority. The initiation was sponsored by a New Orleans chapter of the sisterhood, Xi Beta.

"I never thought a day like this would come," Annabel said, smiling. "I thought I'd always be on the outside, didn't you?"

Joey nodded.

In 1948, the year Joey arrived at Carville, several Beta Sigma Phi sisters started taking trips to the leprosarium to help entertain the patients with shows, cocktail hours, and parties. Soon more sisters joined them, and they made visiting Carville an official part of the sorority's service project. Over the years, the sisters got to know the more outgoing patients like Joey and Ann well. They learned about their lives behind the barbed wire, how they felt about the outside world, their dreams of someday leaving the hospital behind.

Most of the sisters had read the articles about Joey's underground resistance work and how she had transformed Tala Leprosarium. But they learned things about her that weren't in the newspapers and magazines. She loved to give permanents and makeovers to the female patients. She never talked about the war unless someone asked. She loved to dress up in pretty clothes.

She wore a white, formfitting sleeveless dress that day, and when the door opened, the two women were led inside, where they were each given a candle and were soon enclosed by a semicircle of twenty Beta Sigma Phi members.

"We are installing these women, not as a favor to them, nor just to show that we have no prejudice toward the disease, but because we feel as active members they will make a real contribution to the sorority, and be a credit to it," said Mary Jane Caruso, Xi Beta chapter's service chairwoman. "We feel it is an honor to have them, and we are grateful they accepted our invitation."

Joey and Ann learned about the plan to "bid" them in May. The previous service chairwoman had launched a campaign in 1952 to try to educate the public about Hansen's disease, to help dispel the mass superstition and fear that had grown around it. So the sorority began keeping a scrapbook about the disease, compiling modern information and the experiences of the sisters who had grown to be friends with Carville patients. In April 1954, they learned that a researcher for the comic strip *Rex Morgan, M.D.*, about a socially conscious family physician, was trying to learn about Hansen's disease for a series of strips. The sisters handed over their scrapbook, but they wanted to do more.

"We talked to the researcher, Vic Ullman, about our desire to do something constructive to prove Beta Sigma Phi attached no stigma to the disease," Caruso said. "Gradually, after talking over our great admiration for both Annabel and Joey, we decided to invite them to become our sisters. We wrote national headquarters, which offered to pay the membership fee for our two friends to show how much they were wanted."

Joey Guerrero with Stanley Stein and two friends at Carville, Louisiana, in March 1955. *Courtesy of Robert Wiygul*

The ceremony lasted just fifteen minutes. One woman read the pledge ritual. Then they pinned Joey and Annabel, gave them the sorority handclasp, and congratulated them. Just like that, the outsiders had 120,000 new sisters all over the world.

Annabel had been at Carville for eighteen years. She had left behind a husband and three children, and her life was a portrait of the nuances of someone segregated for nearly two decades. Her kids were grown and she had grandchildren now, but she had chosen to make Carville her home in the days when the chance of ever leaving looked bleak. She remarried a fellow patient, who built them a lovely house out of an old chicken coop. She threw parties, went to church, and worked as managing editor of the *Star*.

Now that a cure was within sight, she was anxious about leaving all that behind and what it would be like returning to life outside the fence. "It is natural to feel dependent on a place like this," she told a reporter for the *New Orleans Times-Picayune.* "Many feel resistant to leave, even after their cases have been arrested because they have become isolated from what we call the outside world. . . . What will my husband and I do when that day comes? True, we have much to bind us here—our home, our work—but we are ready and willing to adjust to another way of life.

"Both Joey and I feel our membership in Beta Sigma Phi will help us to adjust when we leave Carville. And it still seems like a miracle to us that we were invited to join."

Joey's disease had all but disappeared, thanks to the new treatments. The monthly tests for the *Mycobacterium leprae* were showing great improvement. But she knew that as soon as she was discharged from the hospital, she couldn't stay in America without a special act of Congress. She was confident, nevertheless.

"I know things will work out," she said.

49

DEPORTATION

James Morrison kept filing his bills, year after year, and those bills kept stalling in committee. The letters kept coming to Carville from the INS, cold and unfeeling and bothersome in their form, calling Joey "the beneficiary" and "alien" and calling her illness a "loathsome or dangerous contagious disease." Each one brought a new wave of fear and horrible allegations. The patient "entered the United States with the intention of remaining here permanently," one said, and she "willfully and flagrantly violated the rules of the Carville Leprosarium by unauthorized travel to various parts of the United States thereby exposing a countless number of innocent persons to the danger and contagion of leprosy."

Joey just kept waking up, hurrying to morning Mass, toast and coffee for breakfast, badminton in the afternoon. Thanking the Forty and Eights for their support, the legionnaires for their dedication, James Morrison for not forgetting about her.

In Manila, Renato Ma. Guerrero of the Ermita Guerreros had achieved national fame as a brilliant and outstanding pediatrician, professor, and chairman of the Department of Pediatrics of the Faculty of Medicine and Surgery at the University of Santo Tomas. He wrote a medical book called *Outlines* and later the *Textbook of Pediatrics for Filipino Students*. He served as president of the Philippine Pediatric Society and was editor of the *Philippine Journal of Pedi-*

atrics and the *Santo Tomas Journal of Medicine*. He worked paces from where his wife had once seen the grenade-blasted body of her commanding officer, the brave guerrilla Capt. Manuel Colayco, who had led the First Cavalry to the prison gates in different days. Rene's letters to Carville slowed and then stopped altogether, and a void opened there over hours and days and weeks and years.

It's impossible to say, based on what remains of the public record, whether the relationship Joey began to share with a new Carville patient much younger than she sprang from love or something more practical, like a desire for American citizenship.

What is known is that by January 1957, Joey had recorded eleven consecutive monthly tests that were negative for leprosy, and she needed one more to be eligible to leave the hospital.

What is known is that Alec Lau was twenty-six, was born in Saigon, Vietnam, had lived in France, and had attended high school and two years of college at the University of Washington before doctors discovered he had Hansen's disease and sent him to Carville in January 1956. He had a father in Cambodia, an aunt in New York City, and he was admitted to the United States in 1951 on a student visa that granted him permanent residence.

What is known is that on January 8, 1957, Congressman Morrison wrote to Joey's lawyer, Robert Kleinpeter, asking if there had been any developments in Joey's case and asking if he should submit another bill on her behalf. And on January 9, 1957, Robert Kleinpeter, who had spent six years working without pay on Joey's case, who had taken two trips to Washington to lobby on her behalf, wrote to Congressman Morrison to let him know he had obtained a divorce for Joey from her husband in the Philippines and would he please include that information in her file "since there was some feeling that if she were granted permanent residence and eventually obtained citizenship, that she might make an attempt to bring her child and husband to this country." Kleinpeter asked Morrison to introduce one more bill and to encourage his colleagues to help move the bill forward. "It is extremely difficult for a country boy to understand why we permit so many displaced persons, such as the Hungarians, and other refugees from Communist countries to seek asylum in this country and eventually obtain permanent residence, and at the same time be so technical and hard on one individual who proved whose side she was on before ever coming to this country," Kleinpeter wrote. "Your interest in this case in the past has certainly proved that you are more than willing to do everything possible to assist Mrs. Guerrero, and I know that you will continue to do so. However, it would be most appreciated by me, as one of your constituents, if a little extra effort could be put forward and obtain relief, not only for Mrs. Guerrero, but for the writer."

What is also known is that on January 10, 1957, a year after Lau's arrival at Carville, Joey Guerrero, thirty-nine, wore an emerald-green silk Henri Bendel cocktail dress and an imported Italian hat embellished with seed pearls and sequins and exchanged wedding vows with the young and handsome Alec Lau before Judge Jess Johnson of Baton Rouge.

And four days later, on January 14, Congressman Morrison's secretary sent a note to his friends at the Baton Rouge morning and evening papers: "Congressman James H. Morrison reintroduced a Bill for the relief of Josefina V. Guerrero on January 14, 1957, which was referred to the Committee on the Judiciary. Joey's marriage to another patient at Carville has been called to the attention of the Judiciary Committee and it is believed that further consideration of her case will include information pertaining to her current marital status."

When the story broke in the *Baton Rouge State Times* on January 15, the wire services began calling and the story of Joey and Alec's wedding flashed to newspapers from New York to Manila. Television reporters showed up, too.

"We just fell in love," Joey told the reporters, "and that was that."

Alec confirmed the explanation with a smile. "That's it," he said. "It must have been destiny."

"It's a free world," said Dr. Edgar B. Johnwick, the medical officer in charge. "I approved Joey and Alec's request."

The story in the *Star* mentioned Joey's wartime exploits and Morrison's new bill, which also had the strong backing of the rest of the Louisiana congressional delegation.

"Joey now has more reason than ever to want to remain in this country as Alec, a Vietnamese, is here on a visa granting permanent residence," the story read. "What of the future? Like all young couples, Joey and Alec have their dreams, hopes, and plans."

Morrison didn't waste any time and quickly fired off a letter to the chairman of the Committee on the Judiciary, pointing out the divorce and marriage and the fact that Joey's new husband had permanent residence in the United States. The chairman then asked the INS for an up-to-date report on Joey. Strangely, much of the callous language present in previous reports was missing from the latest.

The beneficiary, whose present name by a recent marriage is Josefina V. Lau, was born on August 5, 1917, in Lucban, Tayatan, Philippine Islands, and is a citizen of the Philippines. She married Alec Lau on January 10, 1957, in Baton Rouge, Louisiana. He was born on January 4, 1932, in Saigon, Vietnam, and is now a permanent resident of the United States. He has been a patient at the United States Public Health Service Hospital, Carville, Louisiana, since January 1956 under treatment for leprosy. The beneficiary divorced her previous husband, Doctor Renato Guerrero, who is a native and citizen of the Philippine Islands, on December 12, 1956, in Louisiana. The beneficiary and Doctor Guerrero have two daughters, ages seventeen and twelve. The youngest daughter is an adopted child and both reside with their father in the Philippines.

The beneficiary is a patient at the United States Public Health Service Hospital, Carville, Louisiana. She is employed as a secretary to the editor of the hospital paper at a salary of $15 to $20 per week and her assets consist of $900 in savings. The beneficiary has received a high school diploma and completed courses in short-hand and typing in the United States. She is now taking a correspondence course in Journalism from the Louisiana State University. She has no close relatives in the United States.

The beneficiary was admitted to the United States on July 10, 1948, at San Francisco, California, as a temporary visitor for a period of six months to receive treatment for leprosy at the United States Public Health Service Hospital at Carville, Louisiana. In connection with this admission, the beneficiary was accorded a waiver of the excluding provisions of Section 3 or the Immigration Act of February 5, 1917, as amended, as they related to the alien's affliction with a loathsome or dangerous contagious disease. She was granted several extensions of her temporary stay, the last of which expired on August 20, 1951. Deportation proceedings were instituted on October 31, 1951, and on August 31, 1953, she was found to be subject to deportation by a Special Inquiry Officer on the ground that after admission as a visitor she remained in the United States longer than permitted. Voluntary departure has been authorized with the alternate order that she be deported if she fails to depart. Although the order of the Special Inquiry Officer was appealed to the Board of Immigration Appeals, the appeal was dismissed.

Doctor Edgar B. Johnwick, Medical Officer in Charge of the United States Public Health Service Hospital, reports that the beneficiary's case is now considered arrested as she has had twelve consecutive negative tests and is eligible for discharge. He states that as her husband

is a patient at this hospital and his case is active, she will
be permitted to remain at the hospital.

It is reported that the beneficiary rendered extensive
valuable assistance to the United States troops in the
Philippines during World War II.

The accompanying note from her doctor said Joey was "ambulatory and free from physical distress most of the time. She retains
normal vision and good function of all extremities. Her skin shows
extensive atrophic scarring which is the result of long-standing leprosy infection. At present time there is not any clinical evidence
of active leprosy. In April 1957 this patient's lepromatous leprosy
satisfied criteria for apparent arrest (i.e., her tests had been negative
for a period of twelve months). Since that time she has been eligible
for discharge from this hospital."

With the bill pending, Joey Guerrero, who had spent nearly ten
years behind the wire at Carville, was finally free to leave.

50

CALIFORNIA

Joey caught a ride to California with friends and stayed with them for a few weeks. In June, she and Alec, who was also discharged, took an apartment at 1565 Fourth Street in San Rafael, California, not far from San Francisco Bay. The weather was just lovely. It was why she chose California. Her job search was challenging, though. She was honest with potential employers about her disease. One interviewer told her that "because of your chronic illness, you would be a risk and I doubt that you will find it easy to get a position," she wrote to a friend. "I am sure something will eventually turn up, but I shall have to fight prejudice and bigotry along with disappointments."

But after a month of responding to want ads in the newspapers, she found a job as a secretary at the Argonaut Printing and Sierra Press Company on Church Street, across the Golden Gate Bridge, where she earned $325 a month. The post office at Carville forwarded her fan mail, which still came in at a steady clip.

"I was one of the army chaplains who knew you thru visits to Novaliches," wrote the Right Rev. Edward J. Schlotterback from Africa. "Recently my brother sent me a newspaper clipping telling of your marriage in Carville. I wish you all possible happiness and will pray for you both. You were always an inspiration to me for courage and good spirit under your affliction, and for willingness to care for all the others."

The INS extended her deadline for self-deportation, giving her another year to try to become a permanent resident. But the letters kept coming.

"While the one is not alarming, it doesn't take away the feeling of threat," she wrote to James Morrison. "I hope this matter will be settled soon and that you will do all you can to expedite it, so that all this harassment will be taken away from me."

Morrison wasn't concerned. So long as he kept submitting bills, he was assured, the INS would not act.

"I am sure you may consider it as a regular notice and no action will be taken as long as legislation in your behalf is still pending," he wrote back.

On Christmas Eve 1958, the company she was working for was sold. It didn't take long for her to find another job, this time at Levi Strauss & Co., and she started January 19. Two weeks later, Alec Lau fell ill and was sent back to the hospital at Carville, with no idea how long he would need treatment. Two weeks after that, Joey got a letter from the INS assistant director for deportation. "Reason for appointment: interview about your case." Again she wrote to Morrison, apologizing for taking up the time of a busy man, asking him to prove to the INS that he had introduced yet another bill before the Eighty-Sixth Congress.

"I am now employed in this 107-year-old firm and I have a fairly good job, a job which I hope to stay in for a long time," she wrote. "So you see, I am gainfully employed. I keep well and my schedule is tight for I commute five days a week, but I want to prove to all who have faith and believe in me that I would never, please God, have to be a burden to this country or to anyone."

Several months later, the INS announced it was questioning the permanent resident status of Alec Lau because it did not know he was suffering from leprosy before his permanent status was approved.

On and on and on it went, never ceasing.

"We, Joey's former coworkers, are warmly appreciative of your efforts in the past on her behalf," Stanley Stein wrote to Morrison,

"and we are sure the countless hundreds of friends of this courageous little war heroine all feel indebted to you for what you are
trying to do for her."

Joey appealed to Secretary of State John Foster Dulles. "I am
writing to you because I am convinced that you are one of the most
influential . . . men in this country," she wrote. "Please, Mr. Dulles,
could you speak for me, and perhaps ask someone in power at Congress to do something about my bill—every year I am threatened
with deportation and it has been a source of worry for me."

With the help of the American Leprosy Missions Inc., Joey
brought her story to a West Coast television show in late 1959,
essentially outing herself. She appeared on Paul Coates's *Confiden-
tial File* with a doctor from India who specialized in Hansen's disease. Her employers at Levi Strauss & Co. knew about her past, but
her coworkers were unaware. The program was powerful.

"Let me tell you this," the wife of a former Carville patient
wrote to the *Star*, "and you can tell everybody at the hospital, that
this little woman, who suffered so much, did more in half an hour
than any doctors or any other human being to understand and not
fear people afflicted with this illness. She spoke so sincerely and so
beautifully that millions of hearts . . . that day, were filled with com-
passion and understanding and shame for their ignorance."

Joey knew the risks. "If I lost my friends simply because they
found out I had Hansen's disease, then they weren't my friends in
the first place, which would make my life less complicated," she
told a reporter. "And yet, perhaps I would make new friends because
of all that."

She did make new friends. A Hollywood screenwriter named
Virginia Kellogg Lloyd invited her to dinner at the swank Hotel
Bel-Air, and they later went to a party at the home of writer Robert
Carson.

Her employers also began to lobby on her behalf. The chairman of the executive committee even flew to Washington to press
legislators to do the right thing. "She is an able and conscientious

worker," wrote R. M. Koshland, personnel manager at Levi Strauss. "She is cooperative, loyal, and also popular with our other employees. I can vouch for her integrity, as well as character. I can think of no one who is more deserving of citizenship than Mrs. Lau."

Morrison introduced bill after bill, H.R. 2412, H.R. 1278, H.R. 5092, H.R. 2960, H.R. 1737. More lawyers joined the fight. Years trickled by with no action, and Josefina V. Guerrero legally became Josefina Guerrero Lau, and when her relationship with Alec Lau ended, she changed her name again to Joey Leaumax, completely losing any bureaucratic connection to the woman who made headlines. She applied for an adjustment status, one final administrative possibility.

"On July 12, 1961, the decision was rendered," her new lawyer, Norman Stiller, wrote to Morrison, "denying the application on the ground that Mrs. Leaumax is inadmissible to the United States for permanent residence in that the United States Public Health Service has certified that she is afflicted with Class 'A' Leprosy. It would appear from this decision that we have now exhausted administrative remedies, although it is true that an appeal can be made to the Regional Commissioner, but inasmuch as this is a medical finding the chances of having this decision reversed is practically nil."

Class "A" Leprosy. The same reason Morrison's bills failed.

Joey appealed anyway. The terse two-sentence response said the decision was final.

Morrison had no recourse but tried again, submitting H.R. 8751, a plea for relief for Mrs. Josefina V. Guerrero Leaumax.

"You may want to call it to the attention of the Immigration Service," Morrison wrote to lawyer Stiller, "in the hope that as long as the Judiciary Committee doesn't act upon it during this session of Congress (which action without doubt would be unfavorable) deportation action might be withheld."

When news broke about what seemed to be the government agency's final decision, phones started lighting up across Washington, DC. Joey's friends staged one last protest, calling every powerful person they knew. Among Morrison's notes is a scrap of paper, a note to calm the callers. "Miss Towne in Immigration here at main office says, for our information: RE Mrs. G, just tell inquirers that as we understand, Mrs. Guerrero is in non-priority status, which means she is placed in the hardship priority. (that's good, no one will touch her)," the note says. "Miss Towne says this woman will never be deported on account of the tremendous publicity Immigration would be liable to."

51

SUNSET

Renato Ma. Guerrero fell dead on December 1, 1962, just before he was to deliver a lecture at the University of Santo Tomas. Stanley Stein published a memoir about his own life in 1963—*Alone No Longer: The Story of a Man Who Refused to Be One of the Living Dead*—and the press called it "a testimony to courage" and "an eloquent plea for understanding." Gen. Douglas MacArthur died on April 5, 1964, at Walter Reed Army Medical Center, and he was buried in a GI casket and ribbonless blouse, conspicuous in their simplicity.

Two months later, in San Francisco, California, Joey Leaumax got a letter from the INS and hurried to share the news with Congressman Morrison.

> I am sure you will be happy to know that I have received my permanent residence card. I was told that after three years, I may apply for American citizenship. At last, your hard work and concern have been rewarded. Will you also convey to your secretary the good news, as I know whenever you were away she wrote the letters and she wrote me cheerful letters of encouragement.
>
> I want you to know that I am deeply grateful of your efforts in my behalf, and for your fight to keep me in

A portrait of Renato Ma. Guerrero. *Courtesy of Cynthia Guerrero*

America. Has it ever occurred to you that in all this time we have never met, and yet I feel as if I have known you all my life. I think you are a truly kind and good man because I am a total stranger to you but you have continuously championed my desire to become an American citizen. It was indeed a hard and arduous climb uphill, but we have reached the top which can only be surpassed when at long last I am allowed to become an American citizen. That will be a great day for me. Three years will soon pass and I shall be prepared for that day.

Once again, thank you for your many kindnesses in the past, for your untiring efforts to put through the bill, for everything that has made possible my stay in America. I have other letters to write to people to whom I owe gratitude, so for today, goodbye, and as we say in Filipino, *marami pong salamat*. I hope to come to Washington one day soon, and when I do, I shall make it a point to come and see you and greet you and it will be a memorable visit for I shall be meeting you for the first time. Kindest, personal regards to you and your secretary.

Then, a surprise. Joey answered the door one day, and there stood her daughter, Cynthia, holding an infant. Her little girl was a woman now. She wasn't tall like her mother expected. They stood about the same height, and the daughter bore a striking resemblance to the mother.

Cynthia didn't know what to expect. She had only the vaguest memories of her mother, of the visits to Tala Leprosarium and the room full of books, but she had always wondered what it would be like to see her again. The family on her father's side did not understand this desire. "Why do you want to meet her?" they asked. "Why would you do that?"

They blamed Joey for leaving the family, for divorcing Renato. Her father cried to the end of his life, Cynthia said, holding out hope for a cure and that his wife would someday return. He'd tried to move on, and he'd had girlfriends but never another deep relationship. He buried himself in his work. Her grandmother, Renato's mother, would speak ill of Joey in Spanish, critical of the divorce. But Cynthia always wondered.

Cynthia took her burden to a priest, who explained that when a person contracts leprosy, when they're forced to give up the things and people they love, when they're sent to the edge of society, they change. Psychologically, emotionally. They are rejected, so they, too, must reject.

"You feel like a social outcast," the priest said. "You feel left out, you feel like you've been ostracized. That is what happened to her. She just wanted to turn her back."

Cynthia's classmates, some of whom had moved to California, had offered to help her find her mother. When her father died, she was trying to settle the estate and had money for her mother from the sale of a lot in Quezon City. She flew to California to deliver the monetary gift.

Joey was thrilled to see them both and doted on the baby, her first grandchild. But, according to Cynthia years later, the baby was ill with diarrhea. "She couldn't keep anything down. We stayed there about a week," she said. "She got so sick, so sick. When you have a baby like that, you get scared." She thought maybe it was the weather. She wasn't sure if she should take her ill child to an American hospital. Her husband suggested she come home. She already had a return ticket. She told her friend to tell her mother good-bye, for she could not bring herself to say it again. And then she left.

"It's not that I didn't love her," Cynthia would say years later in her little home on the outskirts of Manila. "It's just that I didn't know her."

She still wonders how a mother could leave her child. There are no signs of Josefina Guerrero in Cynthia's home, no photographs or letters or Christmas cards. She has one photograph of her father, and she is proud that he is still remembered with an annual lecture at the University of Santo Tomas. Her feelings about her mother are more complicated.

"Maybe her sickness affected the mind," Cynthia said.

The nuns used to remind her not to hate. She said she does not harbor any hard feelings, but the hurt is always there, even in her old age.

"We're all bidding the world good-bye, I suppose."

52

DISAPPEAR

She was leaving a diminishing trace that she had walked the earth, that she had done great things and was recognized for them. She was tiring of being recognized, because with the recognition sometimes came judgment. She wanted to cast off her old life and try anew.

The final public attention she'd receive on a scale larger than a church bulletin came in late 1967, in the pages of the *San Francisco Chronicle* in a story penned by William Cooney. Joey Guerrero Leaumax, diminutive Filipino war heroine and former Carville patient, had finally gained US citizenship. It had taken a grateful country twenty years to tell the leper spy, yes, you may live here.

She spoke of giving food and medicine and cigarettes to the men on the Bataan Death March and taking the same supplies to prisoners at Los Baños and Santo Tomas. The story recalled her intrepid journey to deliver the minefield map to the Thirty-Seventh Infantry Division, but she was hesitant to talk about it.

"I really don't like to talk about it," she said. "I have almost forgotten."

When she finally told the story, it was not embellished by ornament. She spoke plainly, just the facts. "They gave me the map and told me to deliver it to Malolos," she said. "I walked, went by banca, and walked. There were snipers everywhere. I hid and walked. And when I got there, the Americans had moved to Calumpit another 25 miles. So I took it there."

There were moments when she seemed to harbor regret. She recalled the Japanese officers she befriended in order to get what she needed for the guerrillas.

"We had to get information from them," she said. "Some of them were very nice. They would show me pictures of their wives and children . . . and there I was sending them to their deaths."

After the story ran, she wrote to the *Star* to say she was now trying to graduate from San Francisco State College, majoring in English with a minor in Spanish. She had worked for several years as a secretary and librarian but decided she wanted to go back to school. She said she wanted to be an elementary school teacher and was working on the campus for the Experienced Teacher Fellowship Program and was hoping to study abroad in Spain. She asked the *Star* to publish her thanks to Robert Kleinpeter of Baton Rouge and Normal Stiller in San Francisco and Congressman James Morrison and all her friends at Carville.

It was the last time she would make headlines. The little woman who kept company with generals and cardinals would soon disappear from the pages of the newspapers and from the minds of most Americans, just like the disease that made her who she was. She would pawn her Medal of Freedom with Silver Palm. Her story would be all but lost, just as she wanted it.

53

I AM STILL ALIVE

In August 1970, Dr. Leo Eloesser began writing letters to his contacts far and wide. He was eighty-nine, living in Mexico, and trying to tie up loose ends. He had not heard from or about Josefina Guerrero since 1948, when he had written letters on her behalf, trying to cut tape to get her to America.

He wrote to doctor friends, priests, officials at Carville, asking if anyone had seen her, if anyone knew her whereabouts. "If she is dead," he wrote, "may I ask you please to return this letter to me at the above address with a note of the date of death?"

A month later, he received an envelope postmarked Madrid, Spain.

> 25 September 1970
>
> Dear Doctor Eloesser,
>
> Dr. Paul Fasal sent me your letter. The reason most people think I have died is because I have tried very hard to efface the past. I simply want to forget it! It was too traumatic and has given me no end of heartbreak. Joey Leaumax is my legal name now—neither Miss nor Mrs. Joey could be a boy's name. When I left the hospital in 1957 from Carville, it took me months to find a job and I was without funds.

Whenever I said I had been in a hospital for ten years, employers looked at me as if I was some ex-criminal—I had to lie about the past to land a job—I began to invent a past. Me, who was so particular about integrity and truth and all the rest. But I just had to do it. It cost me money, time and grit to convince Uncle Sam I could be a first-rate citizen. No, I was an ex-patient, not good enough to be a US citizen. But finally, I became one. I also went hungry a good many times because I got fired from jobs whenever the past cropped up. (Can you imagine being hungry after WWII was over?) I was broke all the time. Then I was hired by Levi Strauss & Co. in the Complaint and Adjustment Department—ironical and amusing—all day long buyers and customers complained and insulted me because I had an accent. At any rate I devised a nice way to pacify them but it is a long story, so I'll tell you another time. The Haases (Walter Haas, president) were informed about me and called me into the office. However, they were very kind and understanding. That was the turning point. However, some of the employees were not very nice. I decided to look for another job with a good working recommendation from Levi Strauss. I became secretary to a vice president in a big bank. Later, I took a job with the International Engineering Corp., a subsidiary of one of the world's greatest engineering constructors, Morrison Knudsen, as personnel in charge of their library. I loved that job and was paid, for the first time, a really decent salary.

It was then that I decided to resume my education. This was in 1965. I applied for a scholarship on the strength of the entrance examination which I did very well. I didn't have enough money. I returned to school and did part time jobs at San Francisco State College, typing, filing, etc. You may well imagine how it was to go back to school after being away 18 years. All my classmates were 19 and 20 year-olds. This was good for me and they kept me on my toes, but my thinking had been dulled and it needed to be oiled and worked on. That freshman year was the hardest, but I came through. In 1967–68 during my junior year, I was selected for study abroad—I had just started taking Spanish but I passed the Princeton test—it cost 1,800 dollars—I got all my savings which was about 900 and applied for a loan to pay the rest (it was a federally insured loan, so I don't begin paying until I teach—it better be soon or I'll be needing a cane to reach school). After a year here, I decided I needed another year if I were to reach that level of understanding and some dexterity in the language. I applied for an extension and was given it. I applied for another loan.

I graduated last June, got my B.A. with excellent grades, 4-As and 2-Bs. Not bad for an old lady, eh? Early this year I made an application to the Middlebury Graduate School in Spain for my master's—I was accepted. That was a gamble because I don't have any money. Unfortunately my application for loan got delayed by the mail strike and it came too late for deadline. I applied for another federally insured student loan and the bank just wrote to say all I can have is $1,000. $850 of that goes to tuition and $150 is not even enough for 3-months room and board. I have been writing people I know asking them to help me out. I need at least 7,000 pesetas to live. Room and board—the least expensive—is 5,500 pesetas, but I'll need books, supplies, laundry, etc. One good friend promised to send me $20 each month and another $10. I am looking for an hour or so a day teaching-English job which should net me at least 3,000 pesetas. The $30 plus the possible 3,000 pesetas is only 5,100 pesetas—not even enough for my room and board. Oh well, something will turn up. So far, the good Lord has provided for me.

I am still alive and full of the zest for life. I hope I will be able to earn my master's—it will be until June here, and from June to September in Middlebury, Vermont, where I will get my certificate. Then, Deo Volente, I may hopefully teach. It will be nice to earn some money again and not to be dependent upon the kind charity of my friends and the loan department of Uncle Sam. I now owe the Student Loan Department over $4,000—when I start teaching they will deduct about $50 each time I get a check. But it will all have been worth it! I am sending you one of my carnet photos—I look horrible in it but these carnet photos never make you look half-way decent. If you want to write me, just address it Joey Leaumax at the above address. I almost forgot, what is it I can do for you? Do tell.

Kindest personal regards,

Joey

Josefina Guerrero, 1970.
Hoover Institution Archives, Stanford, California.

54

ANONYMOUS

If you could slow down that last morning, June 18, 1996, as she lay dying quiet and alone in the bustling capital of a country that had forgotten who she was and what she had done, if you could reverse the record of her seventy-eight years and spin it backward with your finger, you might start to see a familiar story arc develop. A woman serving others, quietly waiting in the wings for her moment to do something great, then standing to the challenge, then being honored and remembered in death.

This is not that story, but if you follow the trajectory backward, you see on her deathbed a woman who had chosen to be alone for more than three decades, who had shucked her given name, who had disappeared completely from the headlines, whose obituary made no mention of the moments that defined her, the fighting of two different but important wars. She had chosen to be forgotten. The three hundred friends and correspondents in her address books had never learned of her origins. No generals sat at her bedside. No cardinals graced her hospital doorsill. You still wonder about heroes. As George Washington University Medical Center faded from her eyes, you wonder if her ears caught the strains of *Daphnis et Chloé* or *Clair de lune*.

See her behind the folds of the curtains at the Kennedy Center, a smile on her lips as the music comes upon her, then kneeling at

Mass at St. Stephen Martyr, then lost in the flows of humanity on the sidewalks of DC. You see her on a park bench in Paris, then London. She pawns her Medal of Freedom for travel money. See her giving books to the children of friends, for she had no children of her own. Before that, see her in the Peace Corps, a volunteer in 1976, teaching at the national university in El Salvador, serving as a professor in the foreign language department, volunteering every Saturday to teach children English at the local parish. In similar roles in Niger, always helping. Then in school in Middlebury and Madrid and earlier in San Francisco, trying to make herself a better citizen. See her receiving word that her daughter has gone back to Manila. See her leaving the hospital at Carville, a place that will soon no longer be of use because of the advancements in treatment that came about during her stay. See her in the newspapers, a woman of culture fighting a disease she refuses to stigmatize. See her bent over a sewing machine, a typewriter, a circular saw. Then she is in San Francisco, framed by a hospital ship and surrounded by the GIs who felt like they owed her their lives. Then she waits in the saw grass at Tala Leprosarium, a place she had come to die but that she had made new. Then she is receiving a blessing from Father Forbes Monaghan, then riding in an army jeep beside Lulu Reyes, then leaving the Ateneo de Manila for the last time, fearlessly fearful.

Then the crack of war, the waft of smoke, the bomb-torn palm fronds on the gray sky, the closing of the eyes of the dead. The ministering angel walks through the cross fire, resigned to meet her savior, the stench of death on her skin. She is greeted by the starved at Santo Tomas, greeted by the GIs with the Thirty-Seventh Infantry at Malolos, greeted by the Japanese soldiers she would betray. She walks thirty-five miles to deliver a map taped between her shoulder blades. She maps the gun emplacements. She stands outside the Ateneo, looking for Father Fred Julien with money tucked into the folds of her dress. She stands beside the dust-and-ash highway, cigarettes and candy in her hands, as the shrunken and starved battling bastards of Bataan stumble past. She stands before her five-year-old daughter, afraid to give her one last kiss. She stands before the doctor, with a prolonged headache, some fatigue, a single blemish on her cheek.

Stuff the bombs back into the chutes and the bullets back into the barrels, rebuild the rubble and retread the tires, and she is with Rene, a promising young medical student, in Manila on their wedding day, the future before them.

She is playing basketball in the schoolyard under the golden Manila sun. She is studying the expression of the jovial nun at Good Shepherd Sisters. She is listening to the music spilling out of a phonograph. She is soft and young and unblemished, imagining that she is Joan of Arc, listening for the voice of God.

ACKNOWLEDGMENTS

———

My sincere thanks go to the following people, who heard me out, encouraged me, offered advice, gave me a place to stay, or otherwise helped shape this book: Michael Kruse, Kelley Benham French, Tom French, Lane DeGregory, Leonora LaPeter Anton, Thomas Lake, Tony Rehagen, Wright Thompson, Paige Williams, Justin Heckert, Kim Cross, Liddy Lake, Mike Wilson, John Timpe, Neil Brown, Bill Duryea, Michael Mooney, Jacqui Banaszynski, Laura Reiley, Scott Lambert, Mark Johnson, Oliver Mackson, Lance Strother, Heather Curry, Tom Curry, Mary Curry, and Tom Bernard.

My agent, Jane Dystel, is simply the best. And I deeply appreciate the crew at Chicago Review Press, including Jerome Pohlen, Lindsey Schauer, Mary Kravenas, and Meaghan Miller.

Thanks to B. J. Alderman and Donald Mounts for their invaluable research assistance, and to Elizabeth Schexnyder, curator at the National Hansen's Disease Museum, who went out of her way many times to help me tell Joey's story. I'm in debt as well to Cynthia Ma. Guerrero-Madrigal and Manuel Ma. Guerrero III for their encouragement and support. Alex Tizon, Dona Lopez, and Rodelio Juanitas helped immensely with arrangements in the Philippine Islands.

I owe my generous family—Asher, Morissey, Bey, and, most of all, Jennifer—for their patience at home and gracious help with research and reporting. I'm lucky and proud to have such great helpers who work mostly for free.

And finally, thanks to Michael Brick, my dear friend and perpetual inspiration. Everyone leaves behind a name, and you most certainly did.

BIBLIOGRAPHY

Allen, Henry. *Fool's Mercy*. New York: Carroll & Graf, 1984.

Aluit, Alphonso J. *By Sword and Fire: The Destruction of Manila in World War II, 3 February–3 March 1945*. Manila: National Commission for Culture and the Arts, 1994.

Aurandt, Paul. *More of Paul Harvey's* The Rest of the Story. Edited by Lynne Harvey. New York: Bantam, 1981.

Civilian Prisoners of the Japanese in the Philippine Islands: Years of Hardship, Hunger, and Hope: January 1942–February 1945. Paducah, KY: Turner, 2002.

Connaughton, R. M., John Pimlott, and Duncan Anderson. *The Battle for Manila: The Most Devastating Untold Story of World War II*. Novato, CA: Presidio, 1995.

De La Cruz, Jesselyn Garcia, ed. *Civilians in World War II: One Brief Shining Moment*. James B. Reuter S.J. Foundation, 1994.

Dunn, William J. *Pacific Microphone*. College Station: Texas A&M University Press, 1988.

Gould, Tony. *A Disease Apart: Leprosy in the Modern World*. New York: St. Martin's, 2005.

Guerrero, Wilfrido Maria. *The Guerreros of Ermita: Family History and Personal Memoirs*. Quezon City: New Day, 1988.

Hastings, Max. *Retribution: The Battle for Japan, 1944–45*. New York: Alfred A. Knopf, 2008.

Hillenbrand, Laura. *Unbroken: A World War II Story of Survival, Resilience, and Redemption*. New York: Random House, 2010.

Holland, Robert B. *100 Miles to Freedom: The Epic Story of the Rescue of Santo Tomas and the Liberation of Manila, 1943–1945*. New York: Turner, 2011.

Hornfischer, James D. *The Last Stand of the Tin Can Sailors*. New York: Bantam, 2004.

Hunt, Ray C., and Bernard Norling. *Behind Japanese Lines: An American Guerrilla in the Philippines*. Lexington: University Press of Kentucky, 1986.

Hurley, John F., and José S. Arcilla. *Wartime Superior: 1941–1945, in the Philippines*. Quezon City: Ateneo de Manila University Press, 2005.

Julien, Fred, and Richard Pezdirtz. *Promises Kept: Memoirs of a Missionary Priest*. Lufkin, TX: Pez-Tex, 1996.

Kazel-Wilcox, Anne, P. J. Wilcox, and Edward L. Rowny. *West Point '41: The Class That Went to War and Shaped America*. Lebanon, NH: ForeEdge, 2014.

King, Gilbert. *Devil in the Grove: Thurgood Marshall, the Groveland Boys, and the Dawn of a New America*. New York: Harper, 2012.

Lorenzen, A. M. *A Lovely Little War: Life in a Japanese Prison Camp Through the Eyes of a Child*. Palisades, NY: History Publishing, 2008.

Manchester, William. *American Caesar: Douglas MacArthur, 1880–1964*. Boston: Little, Brown, 1978.

Monaghan, Forbes J. *Under the Red Sun: A Letter from Manila*. New York: Declan X. McMullen, 1946.

Monahan, Evelyn, and Rosemary Neidel-Greenlee. *All This Hell: U.S. Nurses Imprisoned by the Japanese*. Lexington: University Press of Kentucky, 2000.

Morison, Samuel Eliot. *History of United States Naval Operations in World War II*. Vol. 13. Boston: Little, Brown, 1975.

Norling, Bernard. *The Intrepid Guerrillas of North Luzon*. Lexington: University Press of Kentucky, 1999.

Norman, Elizabeth M. *We Band of Angels: The Untold Story of the American Women Trapped on Bataan*. New York: Random House, 1999.

Norman, Michael, and Elizabeth M. Norman. *Tears in the Darkness: The Story of the Bataan Death March and Its Aftermath*. New York: Farrar, Straus & Giroux, 2009.

Ohl, John Kennedy. *Minuteman: The Military Career of General Robert S. Beightler*. Boulder, CO: Lynne Rienner, 2001.

Ramsey, Edwin Price, and Stephen J. Rivele. *Lieutenant Ramsey's War: From Horse Soldier to Guerrilla Commander*. New York: Knightsbridge, 1990.

Raymond, Steve, and Mike Pride. *Too Dead to Die: A Memoir of Bataan and Beyond*. Concord, NH: Plaidswede, 2006.

Rottman, Gordon L., and Ian Palmer. *Japanese Pacific Island Defenses 1941–45*. Oxford: Osprey, 2003.

Schaefer, Chris. *Bataan Diary: An American Family in World War II, 1941–1945*. Houston: Riverview, 2004.

Sledge, E. B. *With the Old Breed: At Pelelui and Okinawa*. London: Ebury, 2010.

Smith, Steven Trent. *The Rescue: A True Story of Courage and Survival in World War II*. New York: John Wiley & Sons, 2001.

Stein, Stanley, and Lawrence G. Blochman. *Alone No Longer: The Story of a Man Who Refused to Be One of the Living Dead*. Carville, LA: Star, 1963.

Steinberg, David Joel. *Philippine Collaboration in World War II*. Ann Arbor: University of Michigan Press, 1967.

Van Sickle, Emily. *The Iron Gates of Santo Tomas*. Chicago: Academy Chicago, 1992.

Volckmann, R. W. *We Remained: Three Years Behind Enemy Lines in the Philippines*. New York: Norton, 1954.

Warner, Jack. *Joey's Quiet War: And Other Nonfiction Readings*. Upper Saddle River, NJ: Cambridge Adult Education, 1995.

Wilkinson, Rupert. *Surviving a Japanese Internment Camp: Life and Liberation at Santo Tomas, Manila, in World War II*. Jefferson, NC: McFarland, 2013.

Wygle, Peter R., and Robert Howard Wygle. *Surviving a Japanese P.O.W. Camp: Father and Son Endure Internment in Manila During World War II*. Ventura, CA: Pathfinder, 1991.

INDEX